Pat Barr

JAPAN

B. T. Batsford Ltd *London*

First published 1980
©Pat Barr 1980

ISBN 0 7134 0578 3

Printed and bound in Great Britain by
Redwood Burn Ltd, Trowbridge & Esher
for the publishers
B. T. Batsford Ltd, 4 Fitzhardinge Street, London W1H 0AH

CONTENTS

ILLUSTRATIONS

1 The Great Buddha (Diabutsu) at Kamakura
2 The Ginza, Tokyo—one of the liveliest shopping-streets in the world
3 The Akasaka district of Tokyo, a typical city-scape
4 The Karamon Gate, one of several highly ornamented entrances at the Toshugu shrine, Nikko
5 A bowman on guard; this colourful, realistic figure is typical of many to be seen at Nikko's Toshogu shrine
6 This splendid, cryptomeria-lined avenue leading to Nikko's Toshogu shrine is well trodden by tourists throughout the year
7 The classical Noh stage, with masked performers, musicians and chorus
8 A traditionally dressed geisha, seated on tatami, is the hostess at a tea-ceremony
9 This view of Mount Fuji, taken from Mount Tenjo, shows the sacred mountain at its peerless best
10 The five-storeyed donjon of Osaka Castle, beautifully reconstructed in the original style of castle strongholds
11 The Ginkakuji, Kyoto's gracious Silver Pavilion, set in a landscaped garden
12 The main entrance of Tofukuji temple, one of Kyoto's many historical religious buildings
13 The massive Todaiji temple at Nara houses the great bronze Buddha that was cast in the eighth century
14 Japan's best-known five-storeyed pagoda—in the grounds of the Horyuji temple at Nara
15 One of the powerful guardians of the eighth century Chumon Gate at the Horyuji temple in Nara
16 A small pavilion in the grounds of the Katsura Imperial Villa, Kyoto, considered the ultimate in Japanese landscape gardens
17 An early-morning street scene in one of the older quarters of Kyoto
18 The entrance to a long-established ryokan (inn) in Kyoto
19 Drying rice on racks at a farm near Izumo
20 A street scene in Kurashiki, a town famous for its canals and unusual museums
21 A Buddhist priest rakes the sand of a temple 'flat garden'
22 Beneath these rafts at Kashikojima hang wire cages full of pearl-bearing oysters

ACKNOWLEDGMENT

The Author and Publishers would like to thank the following for supplying the black and white illustrations:
J. Allan Cash, 2, 5, 10; Douglas Dickins, 1, 3, 4, 6, 8, 9, 11, 12, 13, 14, 15, 16, 17, 18, 19, 20, 22; Japan Information Centre, London, 7; and Outlook Films, 21.

Amami Islands

Okinawa Islands

OKINAWA

Naha

KOREA STRAIT

Matsue

HONSHU

Hirado

Shimonoseki

HIROSHIMA

Fukuyama Kurashiki Himeji

Biwa-ko

KYOTO

Ta

FUKUOKA

KOBE

NAG

Beppu

Takamatsu

OSAKA

Otsu

NAGASAKI

Aso
Nat. Park

Tokushima

Nara

Ise

Tob

KUMAMOTO

Ise shim
Nat. Park

SHIKOKU

KAGOSHIMA

KYUSHU

SEA OF
OKHOTSK

• Sapporo

HOKKAIDO

• Hakodate

SEA OF JAPAN

• Aomori
Hirosaki
• Towada

• Akita

SENDAI

n Alps
ark
Nikko Nat. Park
Chuzenji-ko • Nikko
akone Izu
ark
iji-san
76 m
TOKYO
ujisawa • YOKOHAMA
wara • Kamakura
himoda Amagi-san
1407 m

PACIFIC OCEAN

Map of Japan

1 THE LAND AND ITS HISTORY

The land

Japan is an archipelago in the Pacific Ocean, decoratively looped along the edge of Asia from north-east to south-west. Its total land area is 377,582 square kilometres which is about one and a half times the size of Great Britain and it supports a population of about 113,000,000. The country is about seventy percent mountainous and it lies within that part of the Pacific zone which is subject to earthquakes and volcanic disturbances. The typical Japanese landscape is therefore characterised by dramatic peaks, narrow steep valleys, short torrential rivers, deep lakes and hot springs. The fertile plains are found mostly along lower courses of the larger rivers and are centres of high population density. Of the country's many unusual topographical features, the most distinctive are the volcanic cone of the fabled Mount Fuji in central Honshu and the chain of five seas linked by channels known as the Inland Sea.

The four main islands of the Japanese archipelago are Hokkaido in the north, Honshu which is the largest, Shikoku, the smallest, which is about the size of Wales, and southernmost Kyushu. There are also about three thousand smaller islands and islets, many of them very beautiful, and the Okinawan islands which lie 685 kilometres off the southern tip of Kyushu.

The whole country enjoys regular and distinct sessions with abundant rainfall, but there are considerable climatic variations between the islands. The winters of Hokkaido are very severe, for example, with heavy snowfalls lasting up to four months; in Kyushu, by contrast, snow seldom falls and the summers are long and hot. This is also true of Okinawa, which enjoys a positively sub-tropical climate with a summer continuing from June till October. Most of the land lies within the temperate zone, however, and the annual average temperatures range from 17 degrees centigrade at Kagoshima in Kyushu to 6.30 degrees centigrade at Wakkainai in Hokkaido. Owing to its location on the Pacific, Japan has a higher humidity in summer than most of Europe and a correspondingly lower one in winter.

Japan is a land rich in all kinds of vegetation; nearly two-thirds of its area is forested, with a preponderance of conifers in the north and broad-leaved trees in the south. Its plantlife is varied, from alpine mosses to sub-tropical palms and ferns which flourish in its southernmost landscapes. As in Britain, Japan's wildlife has diminished in quantity and diversity during the past two hundred years and the people are now alert to the need for conservation of rarer species of birds and animals such as the brown bears of Hokkaido.

Japan produces a greater variety of food crops than most temperate countries—from the grains and pulses of the north to the rice, sweet potatoes and soft fruits of the deep south. Owing to the scarcity of flat pasture land, livestock rearing is still carried out on a relatively small scale, but is increasing recently as the people acquire a taste for more meat and dairy products. In the past, the Japanese got most of their protein from the sea—including seaweed, of which they make much culinary use. Their ability to provide a versatile series of raw and cooked fish and seafood dishes is unsurpassed. Naturally, the Japanese have always been skilled and diligent fishermen and today Japan is one of the leading maritime nations in the world. The terrain is not rich in minerals however, though there are some reserves of coal and hydro-power.

The historical context

Among the highly advanced ancient civilisations of the world, Japan has always been one of the most isolated. Separated from its nearest neighbour, Korea, by a 160-kilometre-wide channel and from China by 800 kilometres of open sea, the Japanese remained relatively untouched and unaware of the great civil wars and barbarian invasions that racked most of Asia and Europe during the early centuries of the Christian era. Naturally and from earliest recorded time, some trading contacts were established between Japan and China—which, by the time of the T'ang dynasty (618-907) was the most powerful and richest country in the world. During the T'ang, a number of China's political and cultural institutions reached Japan via Korea; the most important single one being Buddhism.

Though managing to steer clear of most international conflict, the Japanese were not long exempt from the strains of civil strife. Early records suggest that, from the beginning of its settlement, the country was divided into a number of warring clans. By the third century A.D. the southern areas of the country, which were the first to develop, were under the control of the Yamato clan, from which members of the present imperial family can trace descendancy. The first recognised capital of the country was Nara, built in the seventh century and an administration and imperial court closely modelled on the Chinese were established there.

About a hundred years later, the court was moved to Kyoto which then remained the national capital for over a thousand years, though not always the centre of authority. From 794 to 1192 was the period of the Heian — the name given to the city of Kyoto at that time — which has since been acknowledged as a golden age for Japan's cultural creativity. It also saw the growth of Buddhist influence and many beautiful temples and religiously inspired works of art were created then.

The leading aristocratic families of the day, who held the dominance of political power, were great patrons of artistic innovations in the fields of architecture, painting, sculpture and literature. Foremost among these noble families was that of Fujiwara, large landowners who eventually took over the reins of power from the Imperial House. Vicious rivalries soon arose, however, between the Fujiwara and other wealthy, powerful families who recruited soldiers to protect their property — these were the original samurai, whose exploits later became the subject of numerous exciting historical dramas and paintings.

As the power struggles continued, the families of the Minamoto and Taira and their supporters left Kyoto to establish their own protected domains in other provinces. In due course, these two clans gained ascendancy and fought prolonged internecine wars against each other, and against the Fujiwara. This time of civil discord, when priests went armed and bands of bullying mercenaries plundered towns and temples, was one of great misery and poverty for most of the ordinary people, who simply wanted a quiet life.

In the twelfth century government by samurai really began. Yoritimo, leader of the Minamoto clan was appointed the sei-tai-shogun (the generalissimo), by the Emperor and it soon became apparent that true control had passed into the hands of a martial shogunate that was headquartered at Kamakura, not far from the present city of Tokyo. The warriors (*bushi*) eclipsed the aristocratic right to rule and their long period of ascendancy was characterised by the warrior ethic and the stark disciplines of Zen Buddhism. The first period of shogunate rule was called the Kamakura period which began about 1192 and ended early in the fourteenth century. Its collapse was partly due to the invasion of the country by the Mongols under Kublai Khan who had invaded north China and Korea. This was the first time in recorded history that the Japanese experienced concentrated foreign encroachment on their soil; they fought the invaders with great courage and eventually defeated them.

Left to themselves again, the warring chieftains continued to compete against each other for political dominance and, for a time, there were two imperial courts—one in the north, the other in the south. Other new centres of population grew up around the feudal castles built as military headquarters for the leading clans—several of which edifices became the focal points for the nation's large cities. This period of conflict, which was similar to developments in Europe at roughly the same time, continued until the sixteenth century. In the middle of that century, a particularly skillful strategist called Oda Nobunaga, a feudal chief, fought his way to a brief military supremacy and began the task of unifying the country, with its headquarters at Kyoto. It was during his lifetime that the first known Europeans, three Portuguese sailors, landed on Japanese soil in southern Kyushu. The year was 1542; five years later the famous Jesuit missionary, Francis Xavier, reached the country from Malacca and for several decades after that the doctrines of Roman Christianity were preached openly in the land.

Nobunaga was assassinated in 1582 before his job of unification was completed, and this was taken over by another leading warrior called Toyotomi Hideyoshi who became shogun and built a large castle at Osaka. Hideyoshi died in 1598 and five years later one of the most famous men in the nation's history, Tokogawa Ieyasu was appointed ruler of the entire country. As founder of the Tokogawa shogunate, Ieyasu wielded power with a very firm hand from his new 'Eastern Capital' of Edo, later known as Tokyo. Ieyasu's achievements were legion; his crest—three leaves of a hollyhock enclosed in a circle—can be seen on many buildings and monuments; his name and his deeds are still indelibly stamped on the minds of the people.

During the early years of Ieyasu's rule trade between Europe and Japan expanded. Two other seafaring nations, Holland and Britain, became interested in this exciting new oriental outlet. The first British trading expedition was headed by Captain John Saris of the English East India Company, who reached Hirado, Kyushu in 1613. Saris was not, however, the first Englishman to reach Japan, that distinction having already been gained by Will Adams, a ship's pilot from Kent who reached the country in a Dutch vessel in 1598. Adams was well treated by the Japanese, though looked upon with great curiosity; he was taken into the Shogun's service and he taught Ieyasu the rudiments of Western gunnery, shipbuilding and navigation. By the time of his death in 1620, Adams had became a wealthy and respected, if still outlandish, figure on the Edo scene.

Ieyasu was fairly receptive to Western technical knowledge and scientific ideas but he became increasingly alarmed by the spread of the Christian faith in his domains. By the first years of the seventeenth century an estimated 500,000 Japanese had been converted by the Jesuit missionaries and in 1614 the first edict against the 'new religion' was issued by Ieyasu's successor. Severe persecution of the Christian community followed and in 1637 Christian believers staged a revolt in Shimabara, Kyushu, which was brutally crushed a year later.

In 1639 — a highly significant date in the nation's history — the Shogun Iemitsu entirely reversed the earlier 'open door' policy towards the rest of the world. Christianity was completely outlawed; the Japanese were forbidden to leave their country and all foreigners residing there were banished from its shores — with the exception of a few Protestant Dutch and non-Christian Chinese merchants who were allowed to continue living and trading in the port of Nagasaki.

Thus began the 264 years of Japan's virtually total exclusion from the rest of the world, during which the great mass of the people remained completely cut off from all foreign ideologies, political encroachments and scientific advances. During this long quiet period no serious disturbance threatened the supremacy of the dominant regime. Power was concentrated in the hands of the shoguns who lived in Edo — which is why the whole period is often referred to as the Edo. The populace throughout the country lived strictly in accordance with the limits imposed by their social class — warrior, peasant, craftsman, merchant. No-one came to the country and no-one left it; technical inventions were confined to the fields of pottery and design, while scientific inquiry of all kinds was discouraged. Commerce consisted of the internal trading of silks, porcelain and rice; history was the study of national achievement and legends of past civil strife; language was solely the tongue of the country, except among the few scholars of Chinese and those permitted to learn Dutch in order to communicate with the Nagasaki traders. Through this narrow 'window on the world' a small amount of information about Western sciences, medicine and technology filtered through to the privileged classes. And little information about Japan and its culture filtered out.

In spite of its insularity, one of Japan's most notable cultural revivals occurred during this period—known as the Genroku, it lasted for about fifty years from the late seventeenth century, and was an artistic renaissance of great vitality and lightheartedness. It was centred on the entertainment quarters of the large cities and was supported by the newly rich bourgeois who had little political power and lived in a state of social subservience to the feudal lords.

The length and totality of Japan's isolation from the rest of the known world at that time is unique in the annals of modern world powers and it undoubtedly consolidated and crystallised the essence of that 'Japanese spirit' which is such an intrinsic and individual part of the nation's psyche even today. But the policy of such deliberately enforced exclusiveness became less and less tenable as new methods of transportation and communication facilitated contact between nations and the mobility of peoples.

By the early decades of the nineteenth century opposition to the restrictive authoritarianism of the Tokugawa shogunate was growing among numbers of Japanese who were increasingly restive at the economic gulfs between the wealthy townspeople and the poorer peasants and lower-warrior classes. Moreover, several foreign countries, particularly Russia and the United States, were determined to penetrate the bamboo curtain that separated Japan from the rest of the world. The actual break-through came in 1853 when Commodore Matthew Perry of the American navy and four 'black ships' as the Japanese called them, arrived in the Bay of Uraga near Edo for the purpose of establishing trade and diplomatic relations with the mysterious unknown orientals.

The shogunate, aware that the country was severely weakened by internal dissensions, circulated copies of the American demands to feudal lords and officials throughout the country, to ask their opinions. The response to this unusual and belated attempt at national consultation was by no means unanimous, but the government eventually decided to capitulate to the foreigners' overtures without any show of force, principally because it was realised that Japanese medieval weaponry would have been little use against any determined onslaught from a modern Western power. So, when Commodore Perry returned to Japan's shores the following year to hear the government's decision and bringing with him a stronger naval squadron very suggestive of American military and technological supremacy, the Treaty of Amity was signed between the two countries. Similar treaties were soon agreed with Russia, Britain and other European powers who had been watching the American initiative with interest, and as a result, nationals of the countries concerned were allowed to reside and begin trading operations in the newly opened treaty ports.

This dramatically abrupt opening of the totally unprepared country to Western encroachments caused deep disquiet and divisions of loyalty within the country. The most active opposition came from the new 'Expel the Barbarians' party which could not bear the spectacle of foreign men (and even a few wives) actually coming to live and work in the hastily erected Western-style offices and dwellings of the treaty ports. During the early 1860s several acts of violence and destruction were perpetrated against foreign residents, and Japanese politicians who were known to be Western sympathisers were also attacked.

Within a year or two of taking up their precarious residence in the country, some European diplomats realised that the Tokugawa government with which they had been dealing was not the sole centre of power within the country and that some of the so-called 'outer clans' in the remote provinces were challenging the mandate of the shogunate. In 1865 therefore, after secret diplomatic explorations, the British transferred their support to those feudal lords who supported the restoration of imperial power and this further encouraged the build-up of a stronger anti-government party with the rallying-cry of 'Honour the Emperor'. Later that year the 'outer clans', headed by the Choshu and the Satsuma, revolted openly against the Shogun. The government armies fought back against the rebels, but were soon defeated while the pro-royalist factions gained in strength. After a series of fairly minor engagements fought with what was, by contemporary Western standards, very primitive weaponry, the supporters of the old regime were finally defeated in battle at Osaka. The last Shogun, Yoshinobu, resigned his office and the Tokugawa family were punished, dispossessed of their lands and forced to leave their capital of Edo. In this fairly brief and bloodless way imperial rule was thus restored to Japan and the samurai-form of government which had lasted since the twelfth century was over.

There was almost unanimous national support for the restoration of the imperial family to power and, in any case, to the vast majority of ordinary people little seemed changed. They saw the revolution as simply the replacement of one group of aristocratic and autocratic rulers by another, more powerful group and the victors did not seem, in the first instance, to be concerned with new political ideals. Nevertheless, the system of rule by Emperor brought great stability to the nation and helped to avert the dangers of further violent conflict simply because the main forces that destroyed the Tokugawa shogunate were already allied to the imperial cause. In this important respect the Japanese situation differed considerably in nature from the many changes in power that occurred in several European and Asian countries at roughly the same period.

Though the majority of the emperors who had reigned during the long period of the shogunate had been little more than titular figureheads condemned to live in powerless, if pampered seclusion in the old royal capital of Kyoto, the young Emperor Mutsuhito proved to be a man of considerable stature and vision. He was given the honorary title of Meiji, meaning 'Enlightened Rule' and when he and the clan leaders of his government took up the reins of power in 1868 it soon became clear that they were determined to thoroughly abolish the standards of the old order and embark upon the full-scale modernisation of Japan. On his formal accession to the seat of power in Tokyo, the new name for old Edo, the young Emperor took an oath that stressed his commitment to '...a search for knowledge far and wide.'

The stable foundation of the Emperor's government and the already proven public-spiritedness of most of its ministers enabled it to initiate many rapid and far-ranging social and political reforms without encountering any organised opposition. The old class divisions of warrior, peasant, craftsman and merchant were officially abolished and the feudal lords agreed to peacefully return their land-titles and much of their power to the throne. Soon the clan structure itself was radically changed and territories were divided instead into prefectures (*ken*) as they remain today. Leading politicians went on grand tours of discovery to the rest of the world and came back full of new Western-style ideas for modernisation and reform.

During the eventful and exciting Meiji era of 'Enlightened Rule' the country changed rapidly and relatively painlessly from an under-developed, inward-looking, feudally divided authoritarian state to a dynamic, outward-seeking, modern world power that rallied to the slogan of 'National Prosperity and Military Strength'. The Japanese responded with lively enthusiasm to the introduction of modern Western techniques in the fields of science, medicine, weaponry and engineering and young intellectuals were fascinated by European philosophical, political and social ideas. Western-style buildings were constructed in the major cities, Western-style schools and academies were opened and such modern innovations as electric lighting, railways, banks and daily newspapers had a tremendous impact on the social lives of the masses.

That the Japanese had most effectively learned some of the lessons the West had to teach was proved in 1905 when, much to the surprise of the major powers, Japanese land and naval forces defeated the Russians in a conflict over Manchuria. Their international reputation was further enhanced during World War I, when they fought on the side of the Allied Powers and became the third-ranking naval nation in the world. The strong Emperor Meiji died two years before that war and he was succeeded by Emperor Taisho, whose dynastic name means 'Great Equity'. Equity was a fairly new word in the Japanese vocabulary and appropriate for an age whose goals were the consolidation of democracy and national unity.

By the late 1920s however, their vaulting ambitions had led the Japanese into the pursuit of increasingly aggressive policies on the neighbouring Asian mainland; most of them devised and implemented by a now-dominant military establishment. Early in the 1930s the efficient and well-trained Japanese army invaded and occupied the major towns and cities of southern Manchuria and set up the so-called independent state of Manchukuo, headed by the former Manchu Emperor of China. From then on political democracy was in suspension in Japan, there was a series of cold-blooded assassinations of moderate statesmen and leading capitalists, and military leaders were in the ascendant; between 1932 and 1941 three of the nation's prime ministers were army generals, another three were admirals.

Although Japan never became a Fascist state along the lines of some European countries, the military establishment increasingly dominated internal policy-making and foreign affairs. It was not surprising therefore that, in 1940, during the early stages of World War II, the Japanese allied themselves with Germany and Italy against the United States, Great Britain and other European powers. The following December, under the leadership of the militaristic General Tojo, the Japanese launched an attack against the United States at Pearl Harbour.

The war that followed was fought on several more or less unconnected fronts. The main division of these was, on the one hand, the land battles that took place in China, South-East Asia and reached to the very frontiers of India and, secondly, the war in the Pacific that was primarily naval and involved the capture of strategic islands in the area. In the early days of the conflict and until the beginning of 1943 the Japanese forces chalked up a considerable number of impressive victories on all fronts. But by the end of that year the tide of fortune was beginning to turn and Japan's military leaders had to rely more and more on the absolutely sacrificial courage and devotion of their men in order to maintain their position, for supplies of arms were running short, the internal economy of the country was deteriorating and the forces aligned against the Japanese were increasingly strong.

From the Japanese point of view, the situation became increasingly precarious with the capture of Saipan in the summer of 1944 which brought American planes within bombing range of their homeland. The 'carpet bombing' of the nation's major cities resulted not only in a lowering of morale but great setbacks in the levels of industrial output. During the final year of the war several efforts towards a world-wide cessation of hostilities were made by both sides until, in 1945, the leaders of the United States, Russia, China and Britain issued the Potsdam declaration setting out their war aims against Japan and leaving it no alternative between unconditional surrender and '...the prompt and utter destruction' of the country. The Japanese disregarded, indeed did not appreciate the full significance of this threat until, in August 1945, the Americans dropped the world's first two atomic bombs on the country—at Hiroshima and Nagasaki. Following the country's immediate and unconditional surrender to the Allied Powers, Japan was occupied by Western troops.

In order to appreciate the full significance of this event for the Japanese it is useful to remember that the country had never before in its history been successfully invaded and occupied by a foreign power. As one commentator has said, it was akin to experiencing a 1066 in 1945. Throughout their previous history therefore the Japanese had been able to select or reject the cultures, the social and political philosophies of other countries and, even at the height of the pro-Western Meiji era, this had meant a considerable degree of rejection. But in 1945 the Japanese were a defeated people, they had no choice but to bow under the rule of their occupiers, most of them American, who remained for the next seven years.

In the event, not a single shot was fired against the occupying forces led by General Douglas MacArthur, and opposition of any kind was insignificant. Partly this was because the order to surrender came directly from the Emperor Hirohito himself and the Japanese still retained the habit of instant and unquestioning obedience to any imperial command; also, the Japanese civilian population had suffered so painfully and extensively from bombing of all kinds that any change could hardly have been worse and relief was mixed with their despair when the Allied occupation became a reality. The national qualities of resigned acceptance of adverse circumstances allied to a sturdy adaptibility ensured that the people survived the hardships, shortages and humiliation of the immediate post-war years with amazing resilience.

The total disarmament and peaceful introduction into Japan of several major social and political reforms under the ruling of a new constitution was completed by 1947. But no sooner was this done than the Americans in Japan were faced with the growing threat of Communist encroachment in Asia from both Russia and China. Consequently, new policies were introduced to help put the Japanese economy back on its own feet and the alarming inflationary spiral which had continued since the end of the war began to subside in 1950.

During that year the Korean War broke out and the dangerous proximity of the new conflict to Japan raised grave questions about its national security. At the same time, the war also served as a great stimulus to the Japanese economy and helped pave the way for the official re-establishment of peaceful relations with its former enemies. The Treaty of Mutual Co-operation and Security was signed in September 1951 in San Francisco between represent- atives of various allied countries and a Japanese delegation headed by Prime Minister Yoshida. However, the treaty was made only with a majority of the formerly allied countries, excluding Russia and its Communist allies and the Japanese had to agree to the recognition of Nationalist China (Taiwan). This meant that for many years afterwards, the question of Japanese relations with Communist countries versus Taiwan has been the cause of great dissension within the nation.

The present Japan
The present form of Japan's government is based on the new
constitution that was drawn up during the early years of the
American occupation in 1946. It is very different in spirit from
earlier political structures when absolute power was wielded by
the Emperor or by a military-backed ruler of some kind. The
present Emperor, Hirohito, was born in 1901 and ascended the
throne in 1926. He is married to the Empress Nagako and they
had two children; the eldest, Crown Prince Akihito, is now
married to Crown Princess Michiko and they have three children.

Under the terms of the present constitution the Emperor acts as
the symbolic head of state; he has no powers relating to
government and performs only certain ceremonial functions. He
is a student of marine biology and his son, Akihito, takes a similar
interest in ichthyology. The women of the imperial family are
devotees of music, Japanese painting and calligraphy.

Article One of the constitution states that sovereign power
resides in 'the will of the people' and great emphasis is placed on
the rights and freedoms of the masses and the respective
independence of the legislative, executive and judicial branches
of the government. These concepts are essentially alien to the
Japanese spirit of the past and it is often said therefore that the
people are still governed more by the traditional principles of
their former authoritarian and patriarchal social systems than by
the imposed rules of parliamentary democracy. As one Japanese
commentator has recently put it, '...we have established a
democratic country based on undemocratic conventions—a
mixture of two extremes.' It is this contradiction that leads to the
sense of dualism in Japanese society to which many foreigners
refer.

Under earlier Japanese social systems women were historically
the more oppressed sex, and the new civil code has given them
equal suffrage rights and legal status with men. The code also
states that marriage should be based 'on the mutual consent of
both sexes' and this has undermined, though not yet completely
abolished, the earlier tradition of 'arranged marriages.' For the
first time in history, Japanese women have an equal right to vote
in elections and ever since this was granted a number of women
have risen to high-ranking offices in the nation's public and
political life. An increasing number are active in the professions
such as law, medicine, accounting and architecture which used to
be exclusively monopolised by men. The number of women in

full-time employment in all parts of the labour force has also risen steadily over the years. In spite of all this, Japanese women have a long way to go before they reach real social, educational and economic equality with men, whereas their European counterparts have a slightly shorter way to go.

From an international point of view, the most important section of the 1946 constitution is Article Nine which clearly states that the Japanese '...forever renounce war as the sovereign right of the nation and the threat or use of force as a means of settling international disputes.' Nowadays, the government interprets this to allow for the development of 'Self Defence Forces' that first grew up as a response to the Korean War during the 1950s.

The supreme legislative branch of government is the Japanese Diet, which is the highest organ of state power. Head of the Diet is a Prime Minister selected from the Diet by its members and supported by a Cabinet of up to twenty Ministers. The Diet is made up of a House of Representatives with 511 seats and a House of Councillors of 252 seats. The former are democratically elected every three years and take precedence over the latter in all aspects of decision-making. The two major parties—Liberal Democrats and the Japanese Socialist Party—roughly represent the principal political divisions that exist between conservatives and non-conservatives. As in most other democracies, several other parties are represented by members whose views range from the extreme left to the extreme right. The three most important and influential of these are the Communists, who are naturally opposed to the country's close links with the United States, the Komei Party, originally the political arm of the Soka Gakkai religious movement and now dedicated to 'middle-of-the-road reformism,' and the Democratic Socialist Party that advocates the creation of a socialist society through democratic processes.

Unlike most other Asian countries in the post-war years, the Japanese have not greatly favoured left-wing parties in either their municipal or national elections and socialists of all varieties have usually accounted for less than a third of total votes cast. It is suggested therefore that most of the major decisions about future national policy are formulated by the tripartite power of the bureaucrats, the leaders of big business and the ruling Liberal-Democratic Party. If so, recent economic trends and voting patterns suggest that this state of affairs may be changing.

On the whole, the Japanese respect the parliamentary system and the rights of those in power to govern, and violent opposition of a serious nature against the government of the day is rare. One such occasion occurred in 1960 when there was a great deal of vocal public opposition to the signing of the new Security Treaty with the United States, and thousands of socialist supporters and students held mass demonstrations against the government of Prime Minister Kishi who was eventually forced to resign. The treaty reinforced Japan's dependence on the United States for military support and for years prevented the Japanese from developing their own economic and diplomatic relationships with mainland China. In 1972 however, Prime Minister Tanaka produced a policy of new rapprochement with the Chinese and held a joint consultation with Chairman Mao Tse-tung in Peking; the result was a normalisation of relations between the two countries whose cultural and historical links have always been close. The Sino-Japanese Treaty of Peace and Friendship which was signed in Peking in 1978 took this process a stage further. For the ten-year duration of the new treaty relations between the two countries have been officially established on a basis of mutual goodwill and security.

Japan's rate of economic growth since World War II is generally called a miracle. Following its defeat, the country suffered acute shortages of goods, essential services and communications were almost at a standstill and inflation was dangerously high. During the later 1950s and 60s however, the government pursued a policy of heavy investment in modern foreign machinery and equipment and the introduction of new, more efficient industrial techniques. For years, workers' wages were kept relatively low and stable, though rates of productivity remained high; as a result, Japanese exports soon proved highly competitive in world markets.

In 1964 Japan relinquished its earlier systems of trade and economic controls and switched to the International Monetary Fund and during the rest of the decade the ordinary people were at last able to satisfy their taste for Western consumer-durables and for cars—though the number of car-owners proportionate to the population is still lower than in other major industrial countries. In line with other advanced economies there has been a recent drastic change in the structure of the working population. Those employed in agriculture and allied industries have declined sharply in numbers and there is a corresponding increase in the service sector, where more than half the total working population is now employed.

As the country's prosperity increased, large-scale programmes for the construction and modernisation of its communications' systems, public buildings, dwellings and industrial complexes have been undertaken throughout the entire archipelago. Living standards have risen dramatically, especially in urban areas though the gap between rural-dwellers and city-dwellers has also increased. The consumer revolution has been characterised, as a government White Paper puts it, '...by the spread of consumer durables, the diversification of consumer life and increases in leisure expenditure.' No visitor to Japan today can fail to notice these developments. The Japanese have been able to sustain these improvements because of their success in the selling of their manufactured goods abroad. For the past seventeen years the country has led the world in the annual tonnage of ships launched and the country's motor vehicle exports continue to increase annually.

Nevertheless, by the early 1970s problems of inflation were beginning to worry Japanese politicians as those of many other countries and in 1973 there was a grave 'oil crisis' within the economy caused by its over-reliance on cheap oil that had been abundantly imported from the Middle East. Since then the national annual rate of growth has been adversely affected by the rocketting world prices of oil and petroleum. In 1976 the government introduced a new economic plan for the second half of the 70s designed to stabilise and balance growth. The four top national priorities it listed are the stabilisation of prices and full employment, international co-operation and improved economic security in matters of energy and raw material supplies.

This last point is important because for many years the country has lacked sufficient reserves of domestic energy and mineral resources to keep abreast of its industrial growth. In consequence it has had to rely heavily on overseas trade and imports millions of tonnes of coal and iron ore each year. With typical resourcefulness however, the Japanese have learned to minimise their disadvantages by streamlining production and operating some of the most advanced and efficient high-speed equipment in the world. The widespread adoption of computer-processing and scientific and technological innovations of all kinds has enabled industry to forge ahead.

In line with its expressed aims of improving the everyday quality of life for ordinary working people, the government has increased public spending on health and welfare schemes in recent years. There are welfare offices in all the main urban areas to service the special needs of the elderly, the physically and mentally handicapped and neglected children. The help given by statuary welfare officers is augmented by various voluntary organisations that are partly supported by local and central government funds. It is appropriate, in view of Japanese traditional respect for the aged, that free medical examinations are offered to all citizens over the age of sixty-five.

Today, the average life expectancy of the Japanese is seventy for men and seventy-six for women and is thus among the highest in the world. Post-war advances in medical research and practice have more or less banished from the scene such poverty-induced diseases as cholera, typhoid, typhus and smallpox that were once rife. On the other hand, the Japanese are now much more prone, as are other highly industrialised populations, to the modern 'diseases of civilisation': disorders of the heart, circulatory troubles, mental disorders, fatalities following traffic accidents and cancer are the main causes of death among the younger age groups of both sexes.

The other great problem of modern industrial society from which the Japanese are by no means immune is that of the pollution and over-exploitation of the environment, allied to a general deterioration in the beauty of both urban and rural landscapes. In the large cities much of the 'old Japan' that was both picturesque and inconvenient has been ruthlessly swept away, to be replaced by highways, factory blocks, skyscraper offices and housing developments that are as bleak and unimaginative in design as those in many Western countries. These heavily built-up areas suffer a very high level of industrial pollution, although since 1975 this has been somewhat improved owing to the implementation of 'the polluter pays' laws that have forced industries to develop effective methods of pollution control.

The over-exploitation and unplanned development of natural resources, allied to the increased population densities in the cities and traffic congestion has resulted in widespread problems of water and soil pollution throughout the central provinces of the country. The Environment Agency set up in 1971 to protect the natural environment and eliminate pollution of all varieties has helped to ensure that the situation is better today than it was a few years ago and more stringent laws have recently been passed to control noise and air pollution and to protect wildlife and the beauty of the natural landscape. Issues relating to health and welfare services and the quality of the environment are gaining in political importance as a growing number of young Japanese voters begin to question the proposition that a continual and rapid increase in the Gross National Product should be the sole and prime goal of a highly civilised society.

2 THE PEOPLE: THEIR BELIEFS AND CUSTOMS

From the time of Commodore Matthew Perry's visit onwards, Westerners have been moved to write copiously about Japan, for the country invariably makes a great impact on all who visit it. Indeed it is claimed that foreigners cannot remain neutral about the place—they either love or hate it. Certainly it is a very distinctive nation, quite unlike anywhere else in the world and its people are, in every particular, thoroughly and characteristically Japanese.

This is not to say however that you will find the streets crowded with those figures that have become almost national symbols in the popular imagination of the West. The swaggering, two-sworded samurai vanished with the shogunate; the beautiful kimono-clad damsels with decorated coiffures and ornate fans are seldom seen in such guise except perhaps at New Year and other special occasions; the few remaining geisha—who are accomplished, well-trained, entertainment-hostesses, not prostitutes—appear only at formal, Japanese-style dinner parties.

Because, for geographical and historical reasons, the country remained so long isolated from the main current of world events and ideas, it has developed an extremely strong culture of its own. Many facets of the national life are unique—it is, for a start, the only country in the world where Japanese is spoken! Many of its cultural pursuits and institutions, though of foreign origin, have been very consciously and thoroughly adapted to suit the national psychology. For, contrary to some people's opinion, the Japanese have seldom been mere imitators of other nations and though they have derived a great deal from the rest of the world, first from mainland Asia, then from Europe and most recently from the United States, they do not do so from any feeling of inferiority. Rather, the Japanese are secretly convinced that they can always improve upon and perfect what they take and convert it to their own special requirements. For the Japanese way is one of intensity and absorption; they are people who take things to their own particular extremes, reduce to the absurd, elevate to the most refined, carry to the ultimate—then swing back again towards the moderate before catastrophe can result.

These traits both fascinate and infuriate most Western visitors, many of whom leave the country in a state of considerable ambivalence, having found so much to love, so much to loathe, so much that is quite unexpected, puzzling and exhilerating. Usually, travellers unhesitatingly commend the Japanese for their unfailing courtesy in all personal dealings, their generally law-abiding attitudes and behaviour, their personal cleanliness (it is the unvarying national custom for everybody to bathe daily), their love of small children and their habitual honesty at every level of money transaction. On the other hand, many are equally dismayed by the national propensity to litter public places and to behave with rude aggressiveness in crowds; they often find living rooms draughty and uncomfortable, food served too cold, and they become irritated by the meaningless responses that the people often make to strangers and their apparent reluctance to take a stand on any issue.

So the over-used world 'inscrutable' fits to some extent, at least from the Western point of view. For instance, most Japanese are outgoing and seem extremely eager to welcome foreigners on an uncomplicated level, though they remain incorrigibly self-conscious and care a great deal about what others think of them. Also, nothing really shakes their basic conviction that they are very superior to any *gaijin*—that is, 'a person from outside' which is their umbrella word for anyone who does not racially belong to the exclusive, closely knit Japanese tribe. Naturally therefore, they are extremely patriotic and it is not accidental that their country is called Nippon, which means 'the origin of the sun.'

They do not thrust their patriotic pride upon a stranger however, for they have been trained from birth to dissemble their deepest feelings and to deprecate their own achievements out of politeness. Nevertheless, the wry, mock-serious and self-deprecatory manner in which some foreigners (especially, perhaps, the British) play down their own country and customs often puzzle the Japanese; for, they feel, patriotism is not a fit subject for levity. They have the habit of inquiring most earnestly whether you like their country, and if you genuinely do, then they never tire of hearing you say so. It is politeness too that prompts the Japanese to habitually mask any show of deep emotion in case it distresses others. So they may smile when recounting the details of a catastrophe or bereavement, but this does not imply any lack of true feeling.

In most of their daily lives the Japanese are naturally gregarious, partly because they have few opportunities for solitude; their country is small, lacking space for individual expansion. So they enjoy going around together in groups, as every foreign sightseer soon realises. School-age children and students invariably travel in crowds and, in later years, people combine in groups for most holiday occasions. The first essential group is the extended family, but there are also groups based on work, on religion, on leisure or sporting interests to which people are bound by firm ties of duty and loyalty that are often of a life-long duration. There is, in short, a very conscious and deliberate group-consciousness at work in all areas of their human relationships and so people try very hard to get on harmoniously and easily with those around them. These voluntary, close-knit groupings give strength and durability to the social framework, though they also contribute to the haunting sense of the irreversible 'us and them' that a stranger usually senses in the country. It is partly because the Japanese satisfactorily fulfil their own needs for social intercourse and friendship in this way that it is not easy for a foreigner to establish close contacts with them.

By our Western standards, the political and social lives of the average Japanese are quite conservative, predictable and constricted. The vast majority will unquestioningly obey the orders of any superior for instance—father, boss, or anyone endowed with sufficient authority. And yet (there is always a 'yet'), they are sometimes prone to seemingly irrational and often violent personal outbreaks, to the over-enthusiastic espousal of radical causes and extreme indulgence in all sorts of passing fads and fashions. They are volatile and restless, avid for new facts, new ideas—which they tend to adopt without much deep understanding. Full of nervous energy, they have always been able to adapt resiliently to every changing time; temperamentally, they are not in the least attuned to the passive acceptance and quietism of the so-called 'unchanging East.'

The Japanese enthusiasm for the new often makes them go overboard for flashy and gimmicky foreign importations, but it is important to remember in this connection that the majority have only recently acquired the wherewithal to indulge themselves very much in any direction. Those born before World War II led lives that were hard-working, spartan and frugal compared to their contemporaries in the West—for example, as late as 1935 the average life expectancy of the Japanese male was forty-seven years, and only a very few had the chance to widen their educational or working horizons. It is perhaps not surprising therefore that the rapid acquisition of material possessions is a prime goal for most ordinary families and that Japanese youth spend their wages easily and lavishly in the pursuit of pleasurable pastimes with a seeming recklessness that would have been inconceivable to their grand-parents, very much as in the West.

Leisure itself is still a fairly precious commodity to the average Japanese worker however, for hours of employment are longer than those in most Western European countries and the average young working male claims to have only six hours per week of pure leisure time. Off-duty benefits and recreational facilities are plentifully provided by all the large companies that most young Japanese aspire to join, attracted by the security of the strong inter-dependence between employers and workers that makes the typical large organisation much more of a 'family' in structure and outlook than its Western counterpart.

Family life itself has changed very considerably in Japan during the years since World War II, and, as in most other countries of rapid economic growth, there is a trend towards greater generational divisions and separations into smaller nuclear family units. The birth rate has declined sharply since 1960 and the average rate is now 18.6 per thousand, resulting in an average family size of 2.7 children. This represents a very dramatic change indeed from the old-fashioned pattern in which several children, parents and grandparents lived together under one roof. Sociologists have noted that this change has reduced the level of family experience and obligation among the young and so allows for their greater mobility and independence. To an extent, of course, this is at the expense of security, loyalty and the psychological benefits of inter-dependent community living.

In spite of these developments Japanese family ties are exceedingly strong by modern Western standards; it is not uncommon, for example, for an elder brother or sister to postpone marriage for several years in order to help finance the education of younger siblings. In spite of post-war legislation designed to give women equal status with men in all areas of public and private life, the typical home is still run in a traditional fashion. This means that nearly all the responsibilities of domestic routine and child-caring are considered to be women's work, even if they are employed outside the home as well. Married women are expected to subordinate their own ambitions and needs to those of their husbands and children and there is a scarcity of child-care facilities.

Visitors to Japan often remark that married women are not expected to complain at the amount of leisure time which most husbands spend away from the home in the company of work colleagues or friends. Significantly, a recent survey into the attitudes of male workers revealed that only twenty-one percent of them said that their greatest satisfaction in life was being at home with their families. Most of this time is during Sundays and it is defined by husbands as *katei sabisu*, that is, 'family service.' The trend towards smaller and more scattered family units has also meant that the problems of caring for elderly relatives is becoming increasingly acute, and women are generally expected to cope with the needs of the old as well as the young.

With regard to the young, their education is given a very high priority within the family at all social levels. Most children seem to naturally develop a high motivation towards educational success at a very early age, and this is quite largely because, as one commentator of the contemporary scene put it, 'Education is to the Japanese what food is to the French and weather to the English, namely a national obsession.' Full-time education for a minimum of nine years is compulsory and the system is unashamedly meritocratic in that it aims to select the most gifted children in the country for the best educational opportunities, regardless (in theory at least) of their sex, creed or social background. In practice however, boys usually get a larger share of family encouragement and resources than girls and middle-class children have the built-in advantages of more cultured and supportive homes. Recently, there is an increasing trend for even ordinary middle-class families to send their offspring to private educational institutions, many of which are of high calibre.

Entry to reputable Japanese schools is highly competitive from kindergarten level upwards and examinations for all age groups tend to emphasise level of actual performance rather than aptitudes. Competition for university places is particularly intense because a degree is a necessary qualification for most well-paid white-collar jobs. Because there is so much at stake, a disturbingly high number of young people commit suicide every year after they have failed entrance examinations.

During the post-war era, educationalists succeeded admirably in their primary aim of turning out large numbers of disciplined, fully trained and highly skilled people in every scientific and technical field and they are the ones who helped to put the nation back on its feet. Quite recently however, some Japanese intellectuals have begun to suggest that such a highly competitive, technically orientated educational system can have deleterious side-effects on many who have to go through what is known as the *shiken-jigoku*—the examination hell.

Religion

Freedom of religious belief is a constitutional right in the country and it is stated in the constitution that 'no religious organisation shall receive any privileges from the State, nor exercise any political authority.' This reflects the fact that the Japanese, like many other oriental peoples are blessed with an easy sense of tolerance for all varieties of worship.

The oldest form of Japanese worship is Shintoism, which is not found in any other country. It has its origins in very ancient indigenous tradition and has been defined by the Japanese themselves as an amalgam of nature worship, tribal cult, hero worship and reverence for the Emperor. Early Shintoism had no formalised system of theology or ethics; the basic principles of its services being simply that of purification of mind and body. During the twelfth century Shintoism crystallised into a philosophical system, though its beliefs are by no means as rigidly formalised as those of most other religions. There are a number of gods in the Shinto pantheon who inhabit the terrestrial and heavenly spheres and manifest themselves in a variety of forms. During the fifteenth to seventeenth century Shinto believers split into several sects and these later became attached to one or other brand of national politics.

In the Meiji era, when the Emperor was still believed to be possessed of divine powers, Shinto was elevated to a national institution with government support. However, in recent years its influence has somewhat weakened and its adherents are split into numerous sects—of which there are about 160 in the country. Nevertheless, the broad tenets of Shinto retain a considerable hold on the people and the 'Way of Shinto Thought' is deeply embedded in the national consciousness. It is estimated that some eighty-three million Japanese today are professed adherents to the faith.

Buddhism reached Japan from India, via China and Korea during the sixth century and, in its early days, its prime appeal was to the nobility and scholar class. Zen Buddhism is an offshoot of Asian mainland Buddhism and has exerted a tremendous cultural as well as spiritual influence on the Japanese since the fourteenth century. It is difficult to define Zen succinctly, for it is neither a formal religion, nor a form of mysticism nor an ethnical philosophy in the Western sense of these terms.

Followers of Zen reject abstractions in their search for enlightenment which they call *satori.* Zen is supremely basic and matter-of-fact; it seeks a return to the true world that is a unique and individual whole. As one master of Zen put it, 'All our understanding of the abstractions of philosophy is like a single hair in the vastness of space.' The disciplined, self-realised, enlightened Zen mind for which every disciple strives goes straight to the core of being. This idea has had great influence on Japanese artists of all kinds who aimed to express the quintessence of their subject through suggestion rather than through faithful reproduction.

Though the essential spirit of Zen—as expressed, for example, in the stark rock and sand gardens of some Kyoto temples and the sparse black and white lines of Japanese *sumi-e* (ink painting)—is not easily accessible to the average Western mind, it is very worthwhile trying to make contact with fragments of the Zen idea, for its influence is lingering and deep. As another Zen master expressed it, 'When water is scooped up in the hands, the moon is reflected in them; when flowers are handled, the scent soaks into the robe.' The Koan of Zen—the riddle-like problems that masters set their students to induce meditation and intuitive awakening—are among the basic Zen texts and are available in many translations for those who seek some insight into the esoteric Zen world.

Today, the beliefs of Buddhists (of all the various sects) and of Shintoists usually co-exist peacefully and it is quite customary, for example, for orthodox Japanese to have two altars in their households—one for each faith to which they pay their respects every morning. They see no contradiction in visiting a local Shinto shrine to express gratitude for a birth, to call in the services of a Buddhist priest for a funeral and to live their daily lives mainly in accordance with the moral guidelines of Confucius— whose ethical system was also introduced to the country by the Chinese. Japanese places of worship are roughly equally divided between Shinto shrines and Buddhist temples, though, on the whole Shinto gets its greatest support from the older, rural elements of the population. There is also a small, but devoted number of Christian believers both Protestant and Catholic; their churches are run entirely by the Japanese themselves, but it is sometimes possible to attend services in English.

The twentieth century has also seen the growth of a number of so-called 'new religions' who now claim between them about eighteen million adherents. Most of them are inspired by the personality of a charismatic leader and attract a diversity of very fervent followers. These religions are not really so startlingly new, for they contain many elements of Buddhism, Shintoism and even Christianity. Their novel factors are their popularised methods of presentation and evangelism and their modern interpretations of ancient moral and spiritual teachings. Two of the most popular are Soka Gakkai, the 'Value Creating Association' and Tenrikyo, the 'Religion of Divine Wisdom.' The former is based upon the teachings of Nichiren, a thirteenth-century Buddhist priest. Its adherents, who believe in strict self-discipline and the union of the religious and national life, are frequently political activists and militant campaigners for their party during elections. Tenrikyo, which was founded by a woman, has a fairly uncomplicated doctrinal base and its followers express an optimistic desire for the coming of the Kingdom of God on earth in the immediate future.

The majority of Buddhist and Shintoist places of worship are open to the public every day, for there is no fixed day of divine services and people pray when they wish, most especially at times of religious festival. It is quite acceptable for foreigners to visit temples and shrines, though there are some temple buildings inhabited by monks for which prior permission must be obtained.

Festivals

The colour and variety of the Japanese seasonal range is celebrated in a calendar of festivals and rituals that are closely associated with the rhythms of nature and, often, with various religious beliefs. Many of them are quite distinctly Japanese in character and are a much-loved part of the national life. The majority of these festivals fall in the months of July, September and October, though, as with the Chinese, the single most important is the New Year. Unlike the Chinese, the Japanese adopted the solar calendar in 1873 so that their New Year is from 1 to 3 January, as in the West. All factories and businesses close during this period and many households are decorated with pine boughs, ferns, bamboo branches, oranges and sometimes a lobster—representing good wishes for a 'long, strong and prosperous' year. On New Year's Eve people crowd into their neighbourhood temples and shrines to pay their respects to the gods, and at midnight bells toll to signify the old year's passing. Throughout the festival there is a general air of jolly activity which is similar to the Western Yule-tide—people put on their best clothes, exchange greeting cards, meet relatives and friends, eat special New Year fare, such as rice cakes (*mochi*), black beans, chestnuts and they drink a sweet, spicy rice wine. Children also receive gifts which, nowadays, are more likely to be model aeroplanes, skis or pop records than the traditional offerings of shuttlecocks, kites or painted wooden toys.

The arrival of spring, which is in late March in the south, through to late April in the far north, brings the flowering of the cherry trees and thousands of Japanese travel many kilometres to their favourite viewing spots—in countryside or park—to admire these delicate blossoms. The *sakura* (cherry) is the prized national flower of the country and its fragile, short-lived beauty well expresses the people's deep sense of the transience and mutability of the world.

The third of March and 5 May are the dates of the girls' festival and boys' festival respectively. On the former day, a number of dolls dressed in ceremonial robes, together with accoutrements such as teacups, furniture and musical instruments are arrayed in tiers in homes where there are daughters. Some of these doll-collections are handed down from one generation to the next and are both rare and costly. During the day, girls visit each other's homes to admire the displays of dolls rather than play with them. On 5 May, families with sons erect wooden poles in their gardens to which are attached cloth or paper streamers shaped like carp—symbolising the virtues of energy, determination and ambition that are considered appropriate to the masculine sex. Miniature figures of warriors, emperors and horses with accoutrements of weapons and drums are displayed in similar fashion as for the girls' festival.

Some of the most interesting and colourful festivals are local in scale and held at certain places of worship or town centres and with a variety of purposes—such as giving thanks for a successful seed-planting or harvest, honouring a local hero or deity. The night of 15 July is the Bon Festival which is widely observed in some form or other, according to the locality. On the evening of the Bon, families light lanterns and go to graves to honour the dead; in some places they sing chants to comfort them, for the belief is that the souls of the departed return to earth on this night.

Perhaps the most famous of all the locally based festivals or *matsuri*, to use the Japanese term, is the *Gion* which is held in Kyoto in July to commemorate the founding of that city. Crowds of citizens throng the streets, singing, shouting, dancing to the music of flutes and drums and following processions of spectacularly decorated floats. Somewhat similar processions, featuring displays by standard-bearing firemen, are held in Tokyo during the first two weeks of October. It is a good plan to watch a *matsuri* wherever you find one, for it brings out the best in the Japanese— with their joyous sense of occasion and genuine love of being together in large groups. Most foreigners feel that *'Kurisumasu'* on the other hand, encourages the worst in the national character. If you haven't guessed, it's Christmas—when every department store has its Santa Claus, tinselled tree, piped seasonal music. On Christmas Eve restaurants and night-clubs are crowded, people dance to the strains of 'White Christmas' and chorus girls, armed with candles, sing popular carols.

Dress
The Japanese have always spent a lot of their income on dressing tastefully and in accordance with a particular occasion. Hairdressing salons and cosmetic counters are always busy and both sexes are very fashion-conscious, particularly the young citydwellers. The article of dress which is so distinctively Japanese as to be almost a national symbol is, of course, the kimono. One of the most elegant female garments in the world, it was first designed in the eighth century and has changed but little since. It is made up of four parts: sleeves, body, gusset and replaceable neckband; it is worn unlined in summer and warmly padded in winter. The sleeves and back of a kimono are often embellished with crests (*mon*) incorporating various motifs such as leaves, petals, fans or birds. In the olden days each family of importance had its own *mon* and this was stamped on its treasured possessions, its dwellings and palanquins as well as on formal clothes.

Kimonos also have several special and expensive accessories. First there is the *obi*, a sash, usually of woven silk and about 380 centimetres long; then there are *tabi*, the slipper-socks with a separate division for the big toe that allows for the insertion of a sandal-thong. The *geta* (clogs or pattens) worn with these are a delightfully simple and (once you are used to them) comfortable form of footwear, consisting of a piece of flat, slightly raised wood, topped with material and held on by the thong. The sound of clattering *geta* is uniquely Japanese, for no other people wear them. To top off the traditional outfit is the *haori*, a long loose-sleeved jacket of silk or wool. Few foreigners can comfortably wear a kimono, but *haori* and *yukata* (the loose, dressing-gown-type robes worn by both sexes) are favourite buys. A useful acquisition, which matched traditional attire but is in habitual use still, is the *firoshiki*, a square of patterned material into which small possessions of all kinds are bundled and carried. Nowadays, it is mainly older women in the provinces who wear a kimono regularly; most young women reserve its use for holidays and special occasions such as New Year. Both men and women usually dress in rather formal Western-style clothes out of doors and often relax in *yukata* and sandals when they are at home.

Food
As with dressing, so with eating—the Japanese have changed their eating habits considerably during the past hundred years, but they have also retained a number of their own individual tastes and customs. For example, all ordinary restaurants now have tables and chairs and many of them are self-service, but in the best-class, traditional establishments food is served on individual trays and diners sit cross-legged on a floor-cushion.

The staple ingredients of the national diet are rice, fish and vegetables and these are used in a number of versatile and attractive ways. Clear soups, fish and vegetables boiled or grilled are everyday fare, as are omelettes, noodles and fresh fruit. A very popular traditional dish is *sushi*, which is boiled, vinegared rice topped with slivers of raw fish, seaweed, vegetables and/or a dab of horseradish. Another favourite delicacy are *matsutake*, the Japanese mushrooms eaten with soy sauce or white fish and prized for their delicate aroma. The most often served vegetable is *daikon*, a variety of pickled radish with a distinctive odour that many foreigners dislike.

Favourite national dishes for most foreigners are the internationally attested *tempura* and *sukiyaki*. The former is a mixture of seafood and various vegetables deep fried in batter and dipped in a piquant sauce before eating. The latter is a delicious dish which, correctly, should be cooked at the table over an electric grill—or, more traditionally, a charcoal brazier. Thin slices of beef, vegetables and chunks of soft, nutritious beancurd are dipped into a sweetish sauce, cooked quickly and eaten at once. Neither of these famous dishes is cheap; for inexpensive native fare, try *soba*, buckwheat noodles served in vegetable broth; *yakatori*, charcoal-broiled chicken pieces, served on a skewer; and sweet rice-cakes. For snacks, there is nothing to beat *sembi*, the spiced rice-crackers that are the Japanese equivalent of popcorn and much better.

Green tea, served without milk or sugar and very hot is the correct and pleasant accompaniment to all genuine Japanese food, and is frequently served between meals and to visitors. The native beer is available everywhere and is quite good, but wine—of the grape variety—seldom is. Domestic whisky, often embellished with foreign-style labels, is also reasonable; imported spirits are extremely expensive. The traditional tipple, which is served on all formal and festive occasions, is *sake*, a fermented liquor made from rice and best served hot in small, thimble-size cups. It is clear-coloured, tastes innocuous and is more intoxicating than one might imagine.

Japanese chopsticks are shorter than Chinese and so easier to manipulate; ordinary wooden ones are only used once. For a proper Japanese meal, great care is taken to ensure that every dish is presented correctly and a variety of small vessels are used— shallow, covered bowls of lacquer or porcelain, long, rectangular or round plates and saucers with a small quantity of food in each. It is considered polite to try everything, but not to eat every last morsel. The presentation and appearance of the food is considered an essential part of its enjoyment.

Clearly then, the preparation and consumption of real Japanese-style meals involves considerable time and effort and, nowadays, most people eat in semi-Western style much of the time. Breakfast cereals, sandwiches, hamburgers, pizzas, hot-dogs and other sorts of international snack-food are always available in the cities, and at the many *kissaten* (coffee-shops) one can get coffee, tea, snacks, cream cakes and ice creams.

Sports

The Japanese sporting world of today also presents a curious mixture of the native traditional and imported Western. So that, while such games as baseball have become a national institution, peculiarly national sports such as sumo, judo, kendo and karate still flourish. Sumo is a form of wrestling that can trace back its origins over a thousand years. Sumo wrestlers are extremely large and fat gentlemen (often renowned for the quantities of beer and food they consume) who live and train in special dormitory-gymnasiums. They are impressive figures when they enter the ring, weighing up to 165 kilograms, carrying lacquered fans and with their hair arranged in the old-fashioned 'winged' style. Before each bout, they parade round the ring wearing embroidered ankle-length aprons; they limber up, throw salt, stamp their feet all in accordance with ancient ritual and in order to create the proper atmosphere of tension and excitement. The object of a sumo bout is for one contestant to push, slap and shove the other out of the ring, and most foreigners find it a rather slow-moving and even painful spectacle. But sumo has a huge following; the most successful wrestlers are national celebrities and a series of fifteen-day tournaments are held six times every year in the country's major cities.

Kendo is another very ancient sport. It is a form of fencing for which the contestants wear padded guards of a samurai fashion and fight with swords made of bamboo strips. The origins of kendo are based on the practical ethics of Confucianism and the contest is more concerned with coolness and presence of mind than the infliction of injury. For this reason, kendo is still taught as a good basic training for many athletes.

Karate and judo (also called ju-jitsu) are more aggressive and appeal to the volatile martial spirit which is another aspect of the complex Japanese temperament. They are sports of self-defence and have gained considerable international popularity in recent years. Of the two, judo is the more refined and highly skilled. In 1956 it was officially designated as a *bona fide* Olympic sport and there are now thirty-eight member countries of the World Judo Federation. Foreigners who are particularly keen to see the excitement and skill of a first-rate judo contest can get permission to visit the exhibitions that are regularly held at the Kodokan, the world-famous training centre in Tokyo.

Sports such as tennis, rowing and baseball were first introduced to the Japanese during the early Meiji period and very early on they took to the last with great enthusiasm: Waseda University sent a baseball team to play in the United States in 1905. The Japanese soon excelled at Western-style competitive athletics also and they were breaking internationl Olympic records during the 1930s. Since the last war, this enthusiasm has revived and it was a great boost to the national morale when the eighteenth Olympic Games was held in Tokyo in 1964—for which, incidentally, a tremendous scheme of urban renewal and motorway building was undertaken.

Today, baseball is the most popular and widely played national game; it is taught in high schools and competition between youthful leagues is fierce. Stadiums equipped with night-lighting exist in every big city and league games are watched by millions on television. There are also several hundred golf courses in the country, for one of the most prized status symbols for the ambitious business man is to belong to an expensive and exclusive golf club. Many of the less high-powered spend their lunch hours practising on indoor golf ranges which are often to be found on the roofs of office buildings. To a lesser extent, the Japanese have also taken to American-style bowling, to volley-ball, table-tennis and badminton — indeed to practically every sport except cricket!

3 THE CULTURE OF THE COUNTRY I

The culture of the country is ancient, rich and subtle and some of its finest aspects are quintessentially and distinctively Japanese. Consider terms like Kabuki, Noh, samisen, haiku, ikebana—all these are cultural developments of such native originality that they are virtually untranslatable into any other language. In consequence, one of the greatest rewards of visiting Japan is to experience and appreciate such pleasures at first hand, for they are not really transplantable from their own soil. So, for example, the version of Kabuki drama that occasionally appears on Western stages is a very thin substitute indeed for an evening at Tokyo's Kabuki-za which is specially designed for Kabuki productions and whose actors are descended from generations of Kabuki performers. Once in Japan Kabuki is an easily accessible tourist attraction; it can also be a theatrical experience of a lifetime.

The Japanese have always been renowned for their original and prolific visual arts and foreign visitors cannot fail to be impressed by the high standards of the visual appeal in their everyday life. Even the cheapest utilitarian objects are tastefully designed with an eye to colour and the qualities of the materials used; parcels are always beautifully wrapped; patterns of the humblest cloth show a subtle awareness of tone and form which is rare in the West; the small corners of ordinary homes and gardens are thoughtfully arranged with due regard to the harmonies of light and shade, of space and shape. There are numerous beautifully displayed exhibitions of art, sculpture and handicrafts of every sort in all the major cities and they are invariably well attended, for the Japanese never seem to tire of just standing and looking at an artistic object.

Painting and sculpture
Japanese art of all kinds is so variously inventive that it is difficult to characterise, but adjectives such as harmonious, graceful, refined and subtle immediately come to mind. The Japanese themselves try to express their artistic ambitions by suggesting

such concepts as *mijabi* (refined elegance), *wabi* (quiet taste), *sabi*, (elegant simplicity) and the haunting expression of *mono no aware* which means the pathos of nature, that is the eternal transience of nature, the doomed freshness of each spring's new growth.

As in other areas of their cultural life, the Japanese have seldom merely imitated the artistic influences—from China, Korea, Europe—that have come to their country, but have eventually fitted them into their own artistic framework. They can trace their artistic development back for about fifteen hundred years and at every stage during this long period some aspect of the national artistic temperament has developed in newly creative and imaginative directions.

To start near the beginning, some of the most interesting objects of early Japanese art thought to be almost entirely indigenous, are the charming little *haniwa* figurines that date from the so-called Tumuli period of the third century A.D. They are models of humans, animals, birds etc. made originally of terra cotta and placed on the grave-mounds of dead chieftains. Though extremely simple in design, they are lively and charming figures and good reproductions of them can be bought.

The placing of *haniwa* on tumuli is generally thought to be an off-shoot of Chinese burial customs and the first great influence on Japanese art was that of China, which came via Korea. The official introduction of Buddhism into Japan in the early sixth century led to the construction of many Buddhist temples in Chinese architectural styles throughout the Yamato Province. Their pagodas and reception halls were adorned with art objects and, under the impetus of the new religious drive, sculptural skills became more sophisticated. Early sculptures of Buddhist deities were worked in bronze and wood and surviving examples of them are mostly to be seen in Nara, particularly in the Horyuji temple, the original of which was built in the Asuka period of the seventh century.

The foundation of the new capital at Nara in A.D. 710 created conditions favourable to artistic development and it became a radiant age for Buddhist-inspired art of all kinds. The Great Buddha of Nara dates from this period and so do many of the Nara-based art treasures, principally sculptural. Some portraiture is still extant from this period too, most of the subjects being priests and rulers, together with large-scale representations of the Buddhist cosmology. From very early times Japanese painters worked mainly in watercolours and/or *sumi* ink and they excelled in the pictorialisation of action and the subtle suggestion of natural landscape. Surviving decorative handscrolls illustrating religious stories and legends and dating from this period are witness to their long-standing skills.

The ornamental and exotic art of the T'ang dynasty in China (A.D. 619-907) had been an inspiration to Japanese artists; after its decline they began to search for more truly national forms of expression in both art and religious demonstration. It was at this time that Esoteric Buddhism was introduced into Japan by Japanese priests who had been to China, and its mystic rituals required a great number and variety of religious images. The teachers of the new sect emphasised the importance of stern self-discipline and its religious objects were symbolic rather than naturalistic. The sculptural style was rather severe and austere, only features such as eyes and hair were decorated and the sculptural figures were softened only by their 'rolling waves' of symmetrically folded draperies. The Golden Hall of the Muroji temple of Nara contains excellent examples of the work of this period, the Heian.

During the later Heian period when the Sung dynasty was in power in China there was rather less communication between Japan and the Asian mainland. The powerful noble families of the day, the Fujiwaras foremost among them, created a taste for a more secular, aristocratic and elegant style in art and their grand dwellings were liberally embellished with paintings and statuary. The making of jointed wood statues was invented at this time— earlier ones having always been carved from a single block. The most noted sculptor, who worked principally in wood, was called Jocho whose surviving sculptures show a perfect sense of harmonious proportion and balance. Jocho was awarded high ecclesiastical rank in recognition of his talent and this led to generally greater respect being paid to sculptural artists.

Temples became more domestic in style during the later Heian and their interiors reflected the current love of extravagant and colourful decoration. Large wall-paintings and triptychs were in vogue, their subjects included idealised concepts of Buddha attaining absolute dissolution of individual existence, and groups of divinities arranged in sensuous and graceful poses and imbued with a poetic conception of nature. Some of these paintings (called *mandaras*) are to be seen in Kyoto and Nara; one of their favourite themes depicts the coming of the Amida Buddha to Earth with a number of minor deities encircling the principal figure. The popularity of the Amida Buddha and the influence of Indian Hinduism are apparent in many of these configurations. It is not possible to attribute most of these art works to a particular individual for they were done by men called *ebusshi*, that is professional secular painters who were attached to the various Buddhist sects but whose names were not recorded.

Purely secular art of several kinds flourished too during the later Heian which saw the introduction of *kana* syllabary in calligraphy and the production of *Yamato-e* painting. *Yamato* was the ancient name for Japan and this term is used to distinguish art that is absolutely Japanese in essence from that which is greatly influenced by Chinese styles. Hand-scrolls and booklets illustrating the tragic histories of the nobility were popular; these picture romance-tales were known as *monogatari* and could be unrolled and read in sequence, rather like a 'moving picture'. The best known example of the genre dating from this time is the Genji Monogatari of the twelfth century which consisted of fifty-four chapters in book form. Only some fragments of the whole still remain but they are sufficient to suggest the charm and beauty of the whole. They are usually housed in the National Museum in Tokyo.

Contemporary with the Genji Monagatari were the Shigizan type of scrolls—lively and elegant line-drawings to illustrate popular legends, for example of a Buddhist monk and his 'flying granary'. *Sutra* scrolls were also popular; they were like poem-pictures on coloured paper with a text at one side and highly ornamental margins decorated, often, with gold and silver leaf. Folding screens and fans were also decorated with secular subjects—legends, birds, natural landscapes for example, and the national love of the allusive and elusive joke can be seen in the invention of the *ashide-e*, the 'reed-manner picture' in which a few words of a poem are scattered in script among reeds in a marsh to form a literary and artistic puzzle.

The setting-up of the new, military-dominated capital at Kamakura had its effect on the artwork of the time. The Jodo sect of Buddhism which promised salvation to all—not merely the aristocratic rulers—flourished and this was also the time when Zen Buddhism reached its ascendancy in the country. A number of Zen Buddhist temples were built around Kamakura and they housed some powerful religious statuary; the best known of these is the Kendo-ji.

The disciplined, forceful doctrines of the Zen exerted considerable influence on artistic thought of the time and resulted in a general move away from the lavish and romantic decorative work of Heian times. Scroll-paintings were often sold in temple grounds and their content was grimmer—for example, fiercely evocative representations of the tribulations that awaited earthly sinners were graphically depicted in the scrolls of Hell, of Diseases and of Hungry Ghosts. Examples of this genre can be seen in Tokyo's National Museum and in some of Kyoto's temples. In addition to the new temples built at Kamakura, the government also undertook the restoration of many of the Buddhist temples at Nara that had been destroyed in the earlier clan wars. The rebuilding was often in a more Chinese architectural style and Chinese-style paintings again adorned their interiors.

The philosophical ideas of Zen continued to be very influential on all aspects of the nation's cultural life until the sixteenth century. Several of Japan's most devout Zen monks visited China and brought back new creative and artistic ideas from the Asian mainland. One of the monks whose name is still remembered today was Sesshu (1420-1506), a pupil of the painter-poet Shubun; his most famous works are the wonderfully evocative screen paintings of idealised autumn and winter landscapes. On the whole, believers in Zen scorned the proliferation of images which had been characterised of an earlier Buddhist age and thus there was a decline in the plastic arts of a religious kind.

It is interesting to note that foreigners and their strange ways became a popular subject for some Japanese artists during the sixteenth century when Portuguese traders and missionaries first reached the country. One of the earliest is a screen painting on gold leaf paper showing goods from southern Asia being unloaded from a Portuguese ship. Later, Spanish and Dutch people also figure on such paintings which were called *Namban Byobu*, that is the 'Screens of Southern Barbarians'. About forty of these are still extant, some forming part of the collection of the imperial household in Tokyo.

Once the government of the country was firmly established in its new capital of Edo under the shogunate, the ruling class encouraged the production of new elaborate artwork to decorate their noble castles and spacious mansions. Painters and craftsmen of the Kano school, that grew up around the artist Kano Eitoku were much in demand and several of them were invited by the Shoguns to live and work in Edo. One who took up the invitation was Tan-yu (1602-74) who achieved a blend of Chinese and

Japanese styles and whose descendants long remained official painters of the shogunate.

The highly ornamental techniques of the Sotatsu school also flowered during the Edo period. Exploring subjects based on Yamato-e ideals, artists produced large numbers of screens and poem-scrolls. Tawaraya Sotatsu's folding screens depicting the Tale of the Genji are masterpieces; they are also imbued with the artist's romantic vision of the aristocratic past. Sotatsu's most famous predecessor was Ogata Kirin (1658-1716), the most outstanding decorative artist of the whole period. The subject of much of his work was the idealisation of natural landscapes and his screen paintings of irises and plum trees are considered his greatest masterpieces; other examples of Kirin's style, equally fine, can be seen in museums of Tokyo and Kyoto.

Essentially the artwork created under the patronage of the ruling Shoguns was what we call 'establishment' in spirit and form, intended to satisfy the tastes and aspirations of the ruling class. Growing up alongside and contemporary with this style were the graphic pictures of the *ukiyoe* artists whose work became very popular during the seventeenth century. By this time, the leading merchants in the cities of Edo and Osaka had become sufficiently affluent to aspire to artistic patronage in their turn. *Ukiyoe* means 'the passing world' and many of the pictures in this genre were originally produced as story illustrations. Their main subjects were the everyday lives of ordinary townsfolk as they went shopping, dining or to the theatre. Popular actors and courtesans became the usual subjects of portraiture instead of the princes and priests favoured by the nobility. Because of its mass appeal, *ukiyoe* artists were always on the fringes of artistic respectability in their own day, though now their work is probably the most internationally known of all Japanese artistic styles.

It was during this time of civil peace and bourgeois affluence that the *hanga* (wood-block prints) also really came into their own, taking for their subject matter the same lively scenes of 'the passing world'. Using extremely clever and original printing techniques, the native wood-block artists, working in conjunction with engravers and printers, produced pictures of complex colours and textures. These bold, vivid prints appealed greatly to the newly rich merchants who, though required by law to maintain an outwardly conservative and humble demeanor in accordance with their low social status, liked to decorate their house interiors luxuriously and spent lavishly in the entertainment quarters of the big cities.

There are many wood-block artists to look out for, among them Masanobu, (1686-1764) and Haranobu (1725-70) who developed his own individual style of *nishi-ki-e*, that is brocade pictures which were prints using up to ten different colour-tones. Haranobu's favourite subjects were slender and lovely young women in everyday surroundings and they are charming masterpieces of subtle line and colour effects. Two well-known wood-block artists who specialised in portraying famous Kabuki actors of the time were Toyokuni (1769-1825) and Toshusai Sharaku, a short-lived artist of the late eighteenth century. The former is best remembered for his great series entitled 'Views of Actors in Roles'; the latter's vigorous style of portraiture is specially popular today because his approach to his subjects was so uncompromisingly realistic.

Another wood-block artist of the period who now enjoys world renown was Kitagawa Utamaro (1753-1806) who specialised in *bijin-ga*, that is 'pictures of feminine beauty'; they are flowing, sensual portraits of young Japanese women and beautifully evoke the rather melancholy, hot-house atmosphere in which such women usually lived. Two of the best-known artists of the outdoor contemporary scene were Katsushika Hokusai (1760-1849) and Ando Hiroshige (1797-1858). The former, who was supremely skilful in the depiction of lively human figures, produced a very famous series of views of Mount Fuji which must be one of the most frequently reproduced print-series in world history. Hiroshige, a master of the poetic and lively evocation of a landscape-with-figures, is best remembered for his series of fifty-five old posting stations along the Tokkaido highway.

The work of the *ukiyo-e* artists exerted a very considerable influence on the French Impressionist painters and became very fashionable in European artistic circles. However the genre lost is popularity in Japan during the Meiji era when most native artists dabbled enthusiastically in Western-style oil painting and, in their turn, came under the influence of French ideas and techniques. One of the most successful artists who worked along these lines was Kuroda Seiki who lived from 1886 to 1924. After making an intense study of Impressionist styles, he used their soft bright colours to depict the subtle scenic effects of his own native land.

Under the influence of a few enthusiastic English, French and American artists and scholars who lived and worked in Japan during the late nineteenth century, the country's first official art academy was established in Tokyo along Western lines. Many of the artists who studied there were interested in formulating new combinations of Western and Japanese art. The artists most usually connected with the formation of a modern style of Japanese painting are Hashimoto Gaho, Kano Hogai, Shinowa Kanzan and, the doyen of them all, Yokoyama Taikan, whose successful career lasted until 1958.

Though the earlier twentieth century saw some decline in native originality and the general social climate was not conducive to artistic experiment and innovation, several interesting East-West fusions began at that time. During the past thirty years there has also been a fascinating revival of wood-block printing known collectively as 'creative prints'. These differ from the original *hanga* in that modern artists invariably cut their own blocks and use a variety of materials, instead of or in addition to wood to achieve their effects; also they draw their inspiration from international as well as national sources. Among the many productive artists in this genre are Kanae Yamaneto and Onchi Koshiro and several members of the well-known Yoshida Hiroshi family.

Other modern Japanese artists can be roughly divided between those who work within the native traditions and those who experiment with a variety of Western-inspired ideas and techniques—with, of course, considerable overlap and interchange between the two. Many younger artists work mainly in the medium of abstract art and use a number of modern materials such as glass, plastic and steel and their appeal is often of international dimensions. There is a permanent and comprehensive exhibition showing the development of late nineteenth-century and recent Japanese art at the Museum of Modern Art in Tokyo.

The performing arts

Theatre

The classic form of Japanese drama, which puzzles many Westerners and makes addicts of a few, is Noh. It was created during the fourteenth century and some of its aspects are surprisingly similar to the drama of the ancient Greeks. It is rarified and slow-moving, relying on symbolism and studied formalism for its quiet, essentially static beauty. The unvarying Noh stage is a square raised platform; at its back is a large panel decorated with a single twisted pine. A bridgeway leads off to the left and is flanked by three sapling pines. There is a chorus which (unlike the Greek idea) takes no actual part in the drama and this is supported by a small orchestra of flutes and drums.

Casts of Noh plays consist of a small number of set characters—heroes, devils, young ladies, old men—and the masks worn to represent these roles are sometimes hundreds of years old and always of exquisite craftsmanship.

A typical performance of Noh consists of four or five plays woven around historical myths and legends and divided by comic interludes called *Kyogen* where clowns, demons and rogues hold the stage. *Kyogen* language is more colloquial than that used in formal Noh and the action includes broad gesture and mimicry, in contrast to the slow, under-stated dance-movements of the main plays. For these reasons, Kyogen are easier for Westerners to understand and enjoy and help to make a visit to the Noh a rewarding, if esoteric, experience. Before going, it is wise to read a few Noh plays, for the repertoire is fairly small and readily available in various English translations. Classic productions of Noh are performed fairly regularly in the country's main cities where they attract small but highly discriminating audiences.

Another form of traditional Japanese drama that is still occasionally performed is Bunraku, a puppet drama consisting of three elements: the recitation of *Jojuri*, a poetic form of epic; a musical accompaniment to the recitative played on a three-stringed instrument called a samisen; and the action of the puppets. These three elements developed separately, and were woven together in their present form during the middle of the eighteenth century. This was the peak time for Bunraku when Japan's most celebrated playwright, Monzaemon Chikamatsu wrote some outstanding human and poetic dramas for it.

Bunraku puppets are large—about a metre high—and dressed in exquisite traditional costumes. Each is manipulated by three men and is capable of considerable diversity of cleverly stylised movement. As in the Noh, Bunraku language is formal and conventional, the action fairly slow, but anyone interested in the development of oriental puppet drama should make a point of seeing it. Bunraku performances are given fairly regularly in the National Theatre of Tokyo and the Asihiza theatre at Osaka—which was the centre of puppet drama development during the eighteenth century.

Nowadays by far the most popular and colourful form of traditional Japanese theatre is Kabuki which is an exciting and skilful amalgam of several performing arts—music, drama, dance,

spectacle and mime. Kabuki evolved in Kyoto during the early
Edo period as a dance form and was first performed by women.
Later, it developed as a kind of popular drama, the main theme of
which were conflicts of love, duty, honour and loyalty among
individuals and in relation to the repressive feudal society of the
past. Men took over not only the male roles but the female parts
too and it has only been in the last few years that women have
begun occasionally to tread the Kabuki boards again. Kabuki's
origins are easily traceable to Noh and Bunraku, but it is less
classical in content and style for it was always intended to entertain
pleasure-loving, middle-class, urban audiences.

A typical Kabuki performance consists of one or two scenes from
a classical play, one or two dance-items, comic interludes and a
'common people's play'. These items are usually quite unrelated
to each other. The plots of the old theatrical repertoire from which
certain scenes are drawn are often intricately interwoven and deal
with historical incidents or legends that are well-known to the
Japanese. So, for example, a typical programme of Kabuki might
include a scene from a play by Chikamatsu Monzaemon, the most
famous Japanese playwright which will be *in medias res* of some
family scandal, saga of revenge or love; the audience, however,
will immediately recognise the nuances of the action and
characterisation and know what has gone before. The next item
may well be a complete two-act play written in comparatively
recent times and usually concerned with the lives and fortunes of
ordinary folk such as merchants, gamblers, wrestlers, lovelorn
maidens or old rogues. The action is quite brisk and the plot often
rather far-fetched, but any dull moments are invariably enlivened
by the appearance of some comic stage character such as a
swaggering bully or a silly coxscomb.

Also included in the programme (which is lengthy) there will
be at least one dance interlude to the accomaniment of traditional
Japanese musical instruments. Sometimes it takes the form of pure
dance, simply expressive of a mood, or of a flower or a season;
sometimes it is of a romantic or comic variety. Dance is a very
important element of Kabuki because it can also be used to link
parts of the main drama such as the conventions of the 'road-
going dances' to describe journeys. There are also special posed
dances that emphasise high points in the dramatic development,
when groups of warriors are fighting for example, or lovers meet
after a long separation. The beauty of the Kabuki dance is really
conveyed through the flowing lines of the actors' elaborate

costumes rather than through the movement of actual limbs.

As the form and content of a Kabuki performance is so different from that of the conventional Western theatre be sure to read the English version of the programme in advance. But, even if the actual story development is sometimes difficult to follow, one cannot fail to be bowled over by the dazzling costumes, the flambuoyant postures and the wealth of scenic effects. The stage is one of the great theatrical inventions of the world; it is very large and it revolves so that the audience can sometimes watch two scenes going on simultaneously as it slowly turns. Also, principal actors often reach it by walking along the *hanamichi*, a raised aisle that leads from the back of the auditorium and allows for a number of prolonged and dramatic exits and entrances. Another unique feature of Kabuki is that all the female parts are played by male impersonators known as *onnagata.* Most of them are descended from families who, for generations, have played women's parts with absolute integrity and conviction. The *onnagata* role is a refined abstraction of womanhood and contains no hint of the bawdy parody of the Western 'drag artist'.

Much of the acting is very stylised—for example, actors adopt classic postures called *mie* during moments of extreme crisis—and the traditional heavy make-up gives them a mask-like appearance. This is intentional, for the make-up is an essential element of the actors' role-playing and varies according to character; handsome young men and ladies have white skins, devils and villains are daubed with red and so on. But in spite of these conventions, which are unfamiliar to the Western theatre-goer, the consummate skill and passion of the acting is such that the extremes of pathos, sadness and joy that form the stuff of the best Kabuki plays are thoroughly and enjoyably conveyed. Kabuki is regularly performed at the famous Kabukiza in Tokyo, at its National Theatre and sometimes in other main cities. Don't miss it; it is a grand, full-blooded theatrical experience.

Western-style theatre with the proscenium arch was introduced into Japan by its early Western residents over a hundred years ago—the first of its kind, The Gaiety, opened in Yokohama in the 1860s, but 'natives' were seldom seen there. The first performance of a European play for the Japanese was given in 1906 and during the early twentieth century translations of Shakespeare, Ibsen and Shaw's plays were quite popular. Nowadays, due to the influence of films and television, foreign plays are highly thought of and often performed in the main cities in Japanese translation. Several interesting theatrical groups who experiment with Western and Eastern dramatic forms have also sprung up, the best known being the Red Buddha Group. Musical reviews, originally of the Broadway variety are also very popular with Japanese business-men and they are performed with great verve and scenic flair.

Films and television

With their inborn sense of the dramatic and visually spectacular, the Japanese took naturally and rapidly to the art of film (and, to judge from any holiday crowd, they must own more cameras per head than any other people). Certainly the Japanese are now regarded as among the world's leading and most imaginative film-makers. A majority of the films are run-of-the-mill historical drama and pedestrian soap operas of everyday urban life; there is also a well-established genre of 'samurai films' that are similar in style and convention to European stories of knights-at-arms or American cowboy movies. The samurai, like the cowboy, is based on historical fact and has become, in the popular imagination, a larger-than-life hero. A famous actor who specialises in such roles is Toshiro Mifune; two of the best directors are Okanoto and Shinoda. Such films appeal strongly to the Japanese who feel that violence and death are essential to a philosophical understanding of life. Other directors, such as Akira Kurosawa, the late Yasujiro Ozu and the younger Yoshishige Yoshida have attracted considerable attention abroad as well as being much acclaimed at home. Kurosawa in particular brings an epic dimension to his films which are often concerned with the morality of the individual who finds himself fighting against social or political injustice. As in other developed countries, however, the rapid spread of television has affected the film industry adversely and quality is often sacrificed to quantity.

For the Japanese have taken with enormous enthusiasm to *terebi*, as they call television, and the national viewing average of about three hours per day is among the highest in the world. In Tokyo and other main cities a variety of television channels are in operation and much time is allotted to programmes of educational and/or practical content, to sports broadcasts and to soap operas in the American tradition. Some English and American films with Japanese sub-titles are also shown. The Japanese Broadcasting Corporation is called NHK and there are commercial and regional companies also.

Music

The first impetus for Japanese music was religious festivals and rituals and it was then performed at court. The most ancient form, with origins in T'ang dynasty China, is called *gagaku*, literally 'elegant music' and played only in aristocratic circles. It is extremely esoteric to Western ears (and to most Japanese) and nowadays is played only occasionally by highly skilled musicians in the Music Department of the imperial household. Music was always an integral part of Japanese theatre and both Noh and Bunraku depend heavily on musicians for their total effect, and for the telling of stories in chanted recitatives.

The traditional musical instruments are gongs, bells, hand-drums, bamboo flutes and three stringed instruments — the samisen, the biwa and the koto. The samisen is a versatile instrument similar to a banjo and, since the sixteenth century, has been used for all kinds of entertainment — in the theatre, in geisha houses, to accompany ballad-singers. The biwa, shaped like a mandolin, is used in performances of classical and traditional music only and the koto, made of paulownia wood is similar to a horizontal zither. Michio Mayagi (1894-1956) was an expert koto player who wrote several fine pieces for the instrument that are available on record and are more accessible than many to Western ears, being in the form of tone-poems. But since the widespread introduction of complicated Western harmonics there has not been much development in the use of the traditional instruments.

The first introduction of Western musical sounds to the Japanese came through the military and naval bands that accompanied the early American and European expeditions, and apparently the people were both fascinated and amused by the sight of men playing trombones and horns. During the 1880s, which was the height of the Meiji-period craze for everything Western, an Academy of Music was established in Tokyo and modern politicians of the day learned to waltz to the tunes of violin and piano.

The Japanese became increasingly skilled and inventive in the fields of Western-style musical composition and performance during the post-war years and there has been a positive explosion of popular interest in all types of foreign music. Today, eight Japanese symphony orchestras perform regularly in all major cities and their solo artists are of very high calibre. Operatic performances are given regularly in Tokyo both by visiting foreign artists and three well-known Japanese operatic companies. The government grants subsidies to several annual musical festivals to encourage new talent among performers and composers. It is estimated that more than half of all the nation's households now possess some form of stereo equipment—mostly playing Western music, from pop to Beethoven, and the Japanese are second only to the United States in the world production of phonograph records. Indeed, many foreign visitors find the people's addiction to blaring pop rather dismaying, particularly as many of the young listen to it outdoors and with little regard to the tastes of others.

4 THE CULTURE OF THE COUNTRY II

Handicrafts

From the very beginning of their known settlement on the archipelago the Japanese began to create objects that were beautiful as well as of utilitarian value and for centuries since then they have been renowned for their refined skill and delicate, elegant workmanship in practically every kind of handicraft and using every kind of material—wood, bronze, clay, cloth, iron, ceramics. The majority of famous Japanese sculptors and artists always tended to cluster in the more populous areas and near temples and shrines where their patrons lived; but, throughout history, some superb Japanese craftsmen have lived and worked in their own local communities and in every part of the country. For there is a very strong tradition of regional and rural craftwork which has been handed down from generation to generation and is still being practised in some remote areas today. Most provincial as well as national museums have interesting craftwork collections therefore; one fascinating comprehensive collection is at the Handicraft Centre in Kyoto where it is also possible to see demonstrations of the making of traditional ceramics or gold-smithing.

As is the case for most countries, present evidence of really early artifacts is scarce, but recent archaeological excavations have unearthed a number of sepulchral mounds from the fourth to sixth century in which objects such as mirrors, bells, earrings and bracelets have been found. Some of these are decorated with line-relief designs that suggest the agricultural community life of the time.

Naturally, craftsmanship developed in accordance with the needs and tastes of the particular time and innovatory techniques were usually perfected by those who had some connection with the wealthier classes. During the feudalistic Kamakura period of military ascendancy therefore metalwork forged ahead and was much prized; elaborately engraved and inlaid swords and armour date from this period.

The increased popularity of the tea ceremony (see p. 66) during the sixteenth century encouraged the making of decorative iron kettles, ornamental lacquer tea boxes and utensils and, most especially, of ceramic tea-bowls. The aesthetic philosophy of the early tea-masters who fostered this development was that the appreciation of a beautiful object was only complete when the object was put to some practical use and this has influenced basic trends in much Japanese design ever since. Ceramic artists of the period vied with each other in the production of the most perfect bowls which were handed around admiringly by the tea-drinkers.

The essential characteristic of the national folk crafts which flourished at this time—when articles and tools for everyday use were all hand made—is known as *shibui*. It implies a subdued, austere, durable and functional quality of workmanship—be it in ceramics, cloth-weaving, the making of utensils and fans. Colours are usually sombre, dark blues, greens, greys and browns and shapes are sturdy and practical. The ultimate and most polished expression of *shibui* can be found in Japanese ceramic art which was originally influenced by Chinese and Korean potters. The first national centre of ceramic manufacture was at Seto near Nagoya and even today *setomoto* (Seto goods) is a synonym for pottery. Until recent times, hundreds of local kilns existed in various parts of the country all producing ware of a destinctively regional quality and using localised techniques of glazing, colouring and design. Nationally famous examples of local ceramic manufacture are the Kyo ware of Kyoto and the Arita ware of Saga prefecture.

Most of the old, small kilns have been supplanted by the modern techniques of mass-production, but there are still several famous ones in operation, especially in Kyushu. One of the most authentic is at Onda, a mountain village in Oita prefecture, Kyushu where a number of families make fine teapots and water jars in a communal kiln. The late and famous British potter, Bernard Leach was greatly influenced in his work by Japanese ceramic artists and through him many of the traditional glaze and pattern techniques filtered through to other British artists who have adapted them to the making of everyday objects such as mugs and casseroles.

The Japanese are also internationally renowned for their elegant lacquerware which was first introduced by the Chinese and then made to supply the needs of the cultured Japanese aristocracy. Gold lacquerware was elevated to a specially fine art during the fourteenth and fiftheenth centuries, when it was considered so superior that Chinese lacquer artists were sent over to learn the secrets of its manufacture. Kyoto has been the historical centre for highly decorative lacquerwork, especially the refined and delicate variety called *maki-e* which is made by mixing gold and silver dust with the lacquer itself.

Perhaps the best known of all lacquer artists was Nayashige Koami who lived and worked in the courts of both Kyoto and Edo during the seventeenth century. But lacquerware was also used by the ordinary people — especially to embellish tables for ceremonial occasions such as New Year and wedding feasts, and the prefectures of Akita and Yamagata were renowned for the excellence of their local lacquer products. The most popular lacquerware of today originated in Iwate prefecture and is known as Hidehara ware; it is usually red or red and gold, on a black ground. As with ceramics, so there is very little locally made, original lacquerware made today, but many of the modern, mass-produced objects are elegant and most imaginatively designed.

A distinctively Japanese use of lacquered wood is for *netsuke,* the carved and decorated toggles that were affixed by a cord to a purse, tobacco-pouch or any object suspended from the waistband of traditional Japanese dress. They were carved from a variety of materials — wood, ivory, amber, porcelain, metal — and represent a great variety of subjects, such as flowers, animals, demons, gods, masks, characters of national legend. Today, *netsuke* are highly prized by collectors for they suggest much that is great in the national artistic genius, being skilfully and delicately made, witty, inventive, lively and also useful.

Literature
The most quintessentially Japanese literary form that is internationally associated with the country is the haiku. A haiku is a miniature poem which is intended to suggest the vastness of the world's beauty allied to what the Japanese call 'the Ah-ness of things' — that is, the melancholy of transience. A haiku has only seventeen syllables and uses the techniques of condensation and well-known association to express its meaning 'in a flash'. At its best, a haiku crystallises a poetic experience, gives a swift, impressionistic record in words (like a single brushstroke of a sumi-painter) to describe a moment of metaphysical illumination or the haunting mysteriousness of beauty and human existence. This can be achieved in many ways — gaily, satirically, charmingly, sadly — but the aim is always to heighten the mood of the moment.

The earliest extant haiku date from the thirteenth century, but they didn't become truly popular as a poetic form until the beginning of the sixteenth century. The most celebrated of many famous haiku writers was Basho Matsuo, an ex-samurai, pilgrim-poet who was born in 1644. Most of his greatest poems were written during the last ten years of his life when he took seriously to the study of Zen Buddhism and concentrated his search for 'Eternal truths in nature and human life expressed with freshness of technique'. Because of their allusive and elusive Japanese-ness, haiku are very difficult to translate and define satisfactorily into other languages, and the many translations that exist are usually very different from each other. Here is just one possible translation of one of Basho's exquisite verses:

> The Old Folly
> The octopus, while summer moonshine streams
> within the trap, enjoys its fleeting dreams

This is typical of Basho's main theme, for he uses the word 'dream' as a synonym of human life and is much concerned with the tensions between reality and illusion. Basho had many admiring followers, among them the 'Ten Philosophers' as they were later called who had been most creatively influenced by his work. The most famous of these are Ransetsu and Kikaku; the latter is specially remembered for his poetic high spirits, as here:

> There a beggar goes!
> Heaven and earth he's wearing
> for his summer clothes

Several famous haiku poets flourished during the eighteenth century, but, like many other native art forms, haiku-writing went into decline during the Meiji period for it was out of tune with the rapidly modernising spirit of the times.

In recent years however, the writing of haiku has enjoyed a considerable revival — many Japanese write haiku purely for enjoyment or to share with their families and friends. Hundreds of thousands of them, all written by amateurs, appear in small poetry magazines and every year a national haiku competition is held on a chosen theme and thousands of entries are always received. The best ones selected are read with great ceremony before members of the imperial family.

In the field of prose writing, there are extant literary works dating from the ninth century onwards. The early ones, called war narratives, were recited to the accompaniment of music and described the violent events of the feudal days when the country was rent by clan strife. Best known of these (and available in several translations) is the *Heikemonogatari*, a doleful narrative concerning the battles and downfall of the Heike clan.

By far the most famous early Japanese novel is the *Genji Monegatari*, dating from the eleventh century, a monumental account of civil life of the period written by a lady of the court called Murasaki Shikibu. It is a complex narrative and is infused with the every-present Japanese sense of *mono no aware* — the transitoriness of human endeavour and the pathos of natural beauty. It has been translated into English several times, notably by the highly regarded Arthur Waley, and is rightly regarded as one of the classics of world literature.

During the Genroku period, when the *ukiyoe* prints came into fashion, a number of writers produced similarly lighthearted picaresque tales of city life. They were gay, satirical, with many acute observations of the money-loving, materialistic spirit of the times. For an introduction to these novels, read the stories of Saikaku Ihara who lived between 1642 and 1693.

During the Meiji period when foreign influences dominated the cultural scene, several authors of note wrote solidly moralistic narratives that were roughly in the tradition of the nineteenth-century Western novel in that they both reflected and commented upon changes taking place in contemporary society. Two of the best remembered authors are Shimei Futabatei and Roka Tokutomi — the latter's family tragedy called *Hototogisu* has been widely translated.

The early part of the twentieth century was not an encouraging time for Japanese writers and intellectuals, but a revival of the literary scene began in the 1950s with a new generation of fiction writers. The most famous, indeed notorious among them was Yukio Mishima, a brilliant and original writer who cultivated his talent in relation to the spirit of the old-style *bushido* (the way of the warrior). Carrying his theories to the ultimate, Mishima committed suicide in 1971. 'The Sound of Waves', 'Spring Snow' and 'The Golden Pavilion' are three of Mishima's best known works, all easily available in English translations. Other interesting modern Japanese novelists are Eiji Yoshikawa, who died in the 1960s, Yasunari Kawabata who won the Nobel Prize for Literature in 1968 and Shusako Endo. The last has been called the Japanese Graham Greene because of his profoundly Catholic pessimism and most of his work is an exploration of Japanese encounters with the West and makes interesting reading for those concerned with the psychology of present-day Japan. His most famous books, called 'Silence' and 'Volcano' are now available in English translations.

A number of prolific poets have flourished from the 1950s onwards and many of them reveal the influence of contemporary British and American poets and are far removed from the older, native haiku tradition. Some have achieved international renown, among them several women, for there has been a renaissance of poetry written by women—a development that is in line with ancient practice, for some of the most acclaimed poetry of the Heian period was written by ladies of the court. Among the prominent names in today's poetry world are Tomioko Taeko, Yumamoto Taro and Tanikawa Shuntaro.

When reading Japanese literature of any kind in translation, the student must remember that the basic concepts of the language are totally different from those of any Indo-European tongue and that it is uncommonly isolated from all the main language systems of the world. Japanese can be written in either Kata-kana or Hira-gana, both derived originally from Chinese characters. Kata-kana is used to transcribe foreign words and is often the first linguistic form taught to children; most publications written for adults are in Hira-gana, which is a rich but very complex form of writing that takes even the diligent Japanese student several years to master thoroughly. In addition to the forty-eight characters of the native script, the Japanese use many Chinese characters. The difficulties of translation can be indicated by the fact that the spoken language is divided into different styles for narrating or conversing and that there are certain set patterns of usage and nuance which are considered appropriate for practically every kind of social relationship. People must be addressed at the correct level of politeness and formality, and there are certain special conversational usages for women. Thus the sentence, 'I am a Japanese' can be correctly rendered in as many as fourteen subtly different ways. The language abounds in honorifics and also has pronounced degrees of pitch.

Architecture and gardens
Architecture
The traditional style of Japanese building was characterised by regularity, refinement and an elegant simplicity of structure. And

a dominant influence in the shaping of its early architectural styles was the same philosophy that infuses much early painting and sculpture—the elimination of the inessential and the crystallisation to the purest aesthetic form. For this reason, wood, which was the commonest building material, was used plain and unpainted, its surfaces simply being polished and varnished to enhance the beauty of its natural textures.

As in many other cultures, indigenuous architecture first developed in response to the need for established places of worship. The best existing examples of truly ancient pre-Buddhist buildings in the country are to be seen at the Shinto shrines at Ise and at Taisha near Matsue. Though these shrines have been rebuilt many times, their simple beauty of original design has been most excellently retained.

Following the arrival of Buddhism in the sixth century, Japanese religious architecture was greatly influenced by Chinese ideas—the oldest extant example of such a Buddhist temple is the Horyuji near Nara, regarded as the most ancient wooden structure in the world. Naturally, buildings made of wood and thatch, as practically every Japanese one was, were extremely vulnerable to wear and tear, to destruction by fire, earthquake and typhoon—so the Horyuji is unique and no domestic architecture of such early date remains.

From the ninth century on, palaces of a rather more splendid kind, similar in style to the contemporary Chinese, were built and Buddhist temples also became more refined, with storeyed pagodas, curved-tile roofs, pillared halls with ornate carvings and eaves. During the Kamakura period when Zen influence was paramount, a number of austere, beautifully conceived temples were built to house monks belonging to that sect. They were specially distinguished by their massive entrance-ways flanked by powerful wooden statues of the guardian gods.

The late sixteenth century brought great advances in the construction of castle strongholds for which much more durable materials of stone and metal were used in addition to wood. Most of the largest were built during the brief period between 1580 and 1610 and some of these truly magnificent structures still survive— the best preserved being the so-called White Heron castle at Himeji. Others have been faithfully reconstructed in ferro-concrete and exactly in accordance with the original specifications.

These noble strongholds, topped with many-storeyed, peak-roofed donjons were tangible reminders to the people of the power of the feudal lords (the daimyo) of the various provinces. They and the castle-towns that grew up round them dominated the surrounding terrain, controlled lines of supply and communication and became the economic, social and administrative focal points for the area. During the later Edo period large numbers of samurai and their families resided in these castle towns and priests of the Buddhist and Shinto faiths also built places of worship there. As time went on too, the palatial dwellings within the forts became magnificently decorated and their large, well-proportioned rooms were the repositories for some of the nation's most splendid paintings, sculptures and craft products.

Apart from the castles, both public and domestic buildings were designed on an everyday human scale; there were scarcely any monumental structures of public emporia. (It is for this reason, incidentally, that the recent growth of skyscraper blocks and huge industrial complexes has changed the landscapes of Japan even more dramatically than in most Western countries.) A few rural farmhouses and merchant homes dating from the pre-Industrial Age still exist, for example in the rural parts of the prefectures of Yamagata, Gifu, Osaka and Iwate in the north. Called by the generic name of *minka*, these attractive, low dwellings have sturdy wooden frameworks, pillars, crossbeams, sunken hearths in the main room, deep roofs of reed thatch or tile. Some of these are now open for tourist viewing and the Japan Tourist Board can supply details.

Western influence on Japanese architecture really began around the 1870s, when foreign architects were commissioned to build many public buildings such as banks, post offices and railway stations. Most of them were in the heavy, solid European styles of the time with scarcely any discernible oriental influence. Later there was a reaction against this and Japanese architects worked along more original lines using the modern materials of steel, glass and cement in conjunction with traditional wood. However, perhaps the most famous building erected in pre-war Japan was designed by an American — Frank Lloyd Wright who built several fine edifices, in particular the Imperial Hotel in Tokyo which was completed in 1921 and survived the dreadful earthquake of 1923.

Recently, most Japanese urban building is of the international block-buster style common to all the major cities of the world. Soaring ever higher, these super-rise towers are totally charmless and undistinguished and have quite destroyed the former low-level soft browns and greys of the old-style Japanese townscapes.

Highest among them is the Mitsui Building opened in 1974 which has fifty-five storeys and is 225 metres high. Two of the more imaginative modern structures in Tokyo are the National Museum of Modern Art and the National Stadium built in 1964 for the Olympic Games.

In the olden days, house interiors, even those belonging to the wealthy nobility, were furnished with elegant simplicity, even though they might contain ornamental screens and wall-paintings. The distinctively Japanese floor-covering called the tatami was first adopted about five hundred years ago; they are closely fitting, soft woven straw mats that always measure 1 by 2 metres and give an air of spaciousness even to small rooms. Bedrooms as such did not exist; people simply spread futon (movable collections of quilts and bedding) on the tatami at night and stored them away during the day. Cooking and heating was done by charcoal stoves; the hibachi, a portable fire-brazier containing glowing charcoal embers was commonly the only form of heat, and this could be supplemented by a kotatsu, a square container for charcoal which is sunk into the floor as a footwarmer.

Paper lanterns, bamboo tables and stools, decorated screens were arranged to attune harmoniously with the seasons and the diurnal variations of light and shade. Reception rooms had a special recess called a tokonama where flower-arrangements and painted scrolls were tastefully positioned. The rooms were fitted with sliding doors and cupboards for the storage of all utensils and the larger houses had verandahs that could be opened or closed off from the outside. The overall effect was one of subdued, unpretentious beauty and house interiors, with their natural materials, integrated perfectly with the garden world outside.

This kind of older-style Japanese house (though inevitably adorned with new items such as kitchen equipment and some chairs) is still fairly common, particularly in rural areas. In cities, an increasing number of Japanese live in apartment blocks or on estates and their house interiors are usually semi-Western, with perhaps a television on the tatami, refrigerators, bathrooms and flush sanitation. They tend to be cramped by Western standards and most families still sleep on futon, for there is little space for bedsteads.

Gardens

The Japanese are world renowned as a nation of gardeners, and a precisely landscaped garden was considered an indispensable feature of every household — at least until the recent growth of urban flat-dwelling. The intention of every properly arranged Japanese garden is to create a scenic composition using various props such as rocks, trees, water, some lanterns and bridges that will duplicate or on some smaller scale suggest a whole landscape. In olden days, the gardens of the nobility were extremely spacious, rather like pleasure grounds, and with elaborate systems for the channelling and picturesque positioning of ponds and streams.

The whole concept of gardening in the Japanese fashion was first set out as long ago as the twelfth century when two famous treatises on the subject were written: the *Emposho* (Book of Gardening) by a priest, Zoen, and the *Sakuteiki* (Book of Garden Planning) by Nagatsune Fujiwara. It is significant that both these books are still regarded as authoritative, for however much the architecture of the country has been altered by foreign fashions, there is no mistaking the Japanese garden. Essentially, the idea of the semi-natural English garden with mixed flowerbeds or an expanse of manicured lawn is foreign to the Japanese aesthetic, for, though they love and admire nature, they have always felt it can be improved upon.

There are various classifications for the types of garden that can be created on even tiny patches of land. The two principal types are hill gardens and flat gardens, each with several grades of formality. The former feature hillocks, often artificial, water and mossy rocks; in the latter, plain stones and sand, stone lanterns and water-basins are the chief decorative elements. Gardens attached to tea-ceremony houses and called chaniwa also have special characteristics, such as moss-covered walks and clumps of concealing bamboos. They are intended to induce a sense of solitude and detachment in all who walk there and are pleasantly secluded from the bustle of the streets. It is pleasant to observe that, in today's crowded cities, the people's traditional love of gardening survives in their numerous landscaped parks and the small hako-niwa (box-gardens) which decorate the entrances of work-places and apartment blocks.

Many of the most famous Japanese gardens are to be found in the precincts of temples and shrines, particularly in Kyoto where there are over fifty listed as being of special attractiveness. There are excellent examples of the hill garden at the Shukkeien in Hiroshima and the Rakurakuen at Hikone, near Kyoto. The most famous of all flat gardens is at the Ryoanji temple garden in Kyoto.

Flower arranging

In older-style Japanese reception rooms and in tea-houses there is always a flower arrangement, called an ikebana. To the Japanese, the arranging of flowers and grasses is of both spiritual and aesthetic significance. Linear perfection of composition, the beauty of singularity and assymetry, allied to an understanding of the rhythms of natural growth and decay are the basics of all ikebana, and the symbolism of time passing is implicit in every good arrangement. Pods or dried leaves represent the past, half-open blossoms or perfect leaves the present, buds suggest the future. Invariably, an odd number of these constituents are used to form an assymetrical design, for the Japanese consider even numbers unlucky. A perfectly satisfying arrangement, it is said, is like a form of plastic sculpture and a good arranger learns the art through the use of fingers and muscles as well as the sensitive perception of eye and mind. Today ikebana is no longer an essential part of every young woman's education, but there are still more than twenty well-known schools of flower-arranging in existence. Information on them is available from the Ikebana International Centre in Tokyo; some schools offer classes for beginners in English. One of the longest-established is the Ikenobo school which traces its origins to ancient Shinto tradition.

Allied to flower-arranging is the raising of dwarf-trees called bonsai, which the people have perfected to an art unmatched in the world. Pines, maples, cherries and cryptomerias are the trees most often used; they are trained, cut and grafted in order to create an aesthetic suggestion of trees grown in all possible environments and the beauty of large landscapes. It usually takes between eight and ten years to bring a bonsai to the desired state of perfection, during which period weights are hung on the branches to make them curve downward and they are tied into artistic shapes. Exhibitions of bonsai are held frequently in all the main cities and are much frequented by businessmen during their lunch-hours.

Tea-drinking

Another cultural feature of the country which is distinctively Japanese is the art of tea-drinking. This is called chanoyu and is an aesthic pastime which consists of drinking mild and fragrant powdered green tea in accordance with the rituals of a particular chanoyu school. The origins of the ceremony date back to the time when Zen monks quietly sipped tea together and the practice then, as now, was loaded with spiritual significance.

The fine details of the ceremony vary according to the season of the year, those present, the degree of the occasion's formality and even the thickness of the tea served. Special and often valuable utensils and bowls are used and guests wear traditional clothes. Each guest empties a bowl of tea and returns it to the host who makes a fresh bowl for every drinker. A perfectly correct tea-ceremony must be conducted in a special tea-room about nine feet square, furnished with cushions, mats, scrolls and an ikebana.

The purpose of the tea-ceremony, which was always taught to Japanese girls of good family, is to teach the participants the virtues of precision, poise, sincerity and courtesy and to induce a sense of quiet tranquillity and contemplative one-ness with the natural world. To facilitate this, there are long, quiet pauses and topics of conversation relating to artistic matters are formally introduced by the host from time to time. This peaceful old ceremony is currently enjoying something of a revival and several tea-ceremony schools operate in all the main cities. Details of these are obtainable from the Japan Tourist Board and it is possible for visitors to watch demonstrations of chanoyu at some of Tokyo's large hotels and in leading department stores. Instructions in the rudiments of the art are sometimes offered in English—but it is not the sort of skill one can acquire in a week.

5 TRAVELLING AND STAYING IN JAPAN

From the tourist's point of view the size of Japan is very convenient. It is among the smaller of the world's developed countries and travel to all parts of it by air, rail or road is relatively fast and comfortable. Moreover, all the major cities and many of the chief tourist attractions of all kinds are to be found on the main island of Honshu, so it is possible to get a very fair idea of Japan by confining your travels to this one island.

The modern political, commercial and cultural centre of the country is Tokyo, the hub of the thriving, dynamic successful nation that has emerged since World War II. If you have only a very short time to spend in Japan, then it is best to base yourself there, visit the national museums and art galleries, the well-known department stores and take some of the many excursions to places of historic and scenic interest that lie within easy reach (see chapter six).

If your chief interests are artistic and historical however, then head directly for the ancient cities of Kyoto and Nara in western Honshu where the richest and finest collections of the nation's art treasures, its oldest and most beautiful shrines and temples are to be seen. The loveliest (though not the least developed) region of scenic beauty — the Inland Sea — lies within easy reach of Kyoto and many of its smaller islands offer glimpses of old-style rural Japanese life.

Whereas Honshu provides the visitor with a very fair sampling of all Japan has to offer, it is still very rewarding to spend some time on the other three main islands, each of which has a distinctive character and possesses certain unique scenic and cultural features. Kyushu, the southernmost, has several areas of spectacular natural beauty with lovely seacoasts, hot-spring resorts and four national parks. One of Japan's most interesting historic cities, Nagasaki, is also located there. Shikoku, the smallest of the four main islands, is comparatively provincial and old-fashioned with several castle towns and magnificent seascapes. Hokkaido, in the far north, is the most recently developed of the islands and therefore has less to offer in the way of historic or cultural attractions, but it is rich in wild scenery, empty spaces and its main city, Sapporo, is distinctive—being both northern and oriental.

Nowadays, and in contrast to the not-so-distant past, Japan is on the main travel routes of the world and flying time by jet direct from London is about fifteen hours. There are also numerous economic ways of combining a visit to Japan with air-travel to other parts of Asia, to Hawaii and the United States. Various passenger ships and some freighters include main Japanese ports in their schedules and cruise ships from Europe and America offer Far Eastern tours by air and ship that can enable one to spend up to three weeks in Japan.

Of all Asian countries, Japan is currently the most efficiently equipped to receive foreign visitors. There is a nationwide, government-financed tourist office network (The Japan National Tourist Organisation) headquartered in Tokyo, and there are special information offices for foreign travellers at Tokyo International Airport and in Kyoto. All the tourist offices provide a comprehensive series of pamphlets, maps and details of package tours written in English about every part of the country and there are also pamphlets detailing hotel accommodation, shopping information, entertainment facilities etc. The main offices also have free tape-recorded information in English about special local events.

Japan enforces the usual immigration, customs and health regulations and tourists must produce tickets for return or onward journeys and evidence of reasonable financial resources to cover their stay. Visitors intending to stay more than sixty days must apply for an Alien Registration Card. However, there is nothing specially restrictive about these regulations and information about them can be obtained from Japanese overseas tourist offices or embassies before arrival in the country.

Spring-time and autumn are generally considered to be the most congenial seasons for a visit but as the climate is changeable and essentially temperate, all seasons have their attractions—and their sudden climatic surprises. If you go in summer, remember that the East Asian rainy season begins in mid-June and lasts about a month; at the summer's end, there is a period for probable typhoons. The extremes of southern heat and northern cold are considerably greater than they are in the British Isles, so you must be prepared for this if you intend to be either in Kyushu in August or in Hokkaido in January.

Whenever and wherever you choose to travel, you will find the natives courteous and obliging and they will seldom bother you in any way. However, you may well have to bother them sometimes, for it is not at all easy to locate destinations because of the lack of street names, numbers and signs in English. In the main cities there are some signs in Romaji, which is anglicised Japanese written in Roman letters, but you cannot count on finding these everywhere. If you get lost, seek directions from younger people who are more likely to know English and more eager to practise it. But it is as well to remember that the overall standard of English comprehension and speech is not high. This is particularly true in the remoter areas, so if you are making for a certain place, try to get it written down in Japanese beforehand. Guide-interpreters can be hired through hotels or travel agents; they are fully qualified in English and other European languages.

Getting around
Internal public transport systems are highly developed, fast, punctual and invariably very, very crowded. Reliable domestic airline services are operated by three main companies, two of which also run air-buses. They link all the large cities on each of the four main islands to each other and there are also direct services to outlying resort areas such as the Inland Sea and the Islands of Okinawa. The major cities and towns are also linked by rail, most of it state-owned; the bullet trains that run between Tokyo and Osaka are said to be the speediest and most comfortable in the world. It is often cheaper to travel by rail than air, and you see more of the countryside—but be sure to look well in advance if you are travelling any distance. Main-line services are provided with refreshment cars and a rather too efficient loudspeaker system which is only in Japanese.

Express bus services link all the main towns and resorts and there are regular pay-as-you-enter bus services within all city limits—be warned, there are no Romaji signs on them. There are reliable underground services in Tokyo, Osaka, Nagoya, Yokohama and Sapporo. Japanese taxi-drivers, significantly called kamikaze, are reputed to be the most dare-devil and reckless in the world. Their fares are high and up to twenty-percent surcharges are made for late-night journeys—but no tipping is necessary. There are good rent-a-care services in the big cities and cars can usually be hired at short notice, with or without

English speaking guides—but they are expensive. The main inter-city highways have now been well modernised, although they are still usually congested. Significantly, the ratio of paved road length per car is only about eleven metres in Japan, compared to twenty-one metres in the United Kingdom. Owners of International Driving Licences can drive freely in the country. In and around major cities road-signs are in English as well as Japanese, but it is difficult to find your way by private car in the remoter areas. Driving is on the left, which is familiar engough, and most (though not all) the road signs are the same as European. Road maps with Romanised names are available from tourist offices and department stores.

There are several special travelling experiences to be enjoyed in Japan—monorails, cable cars and hydrofoils for example. But do not count on the leisurely romance of a rickshaw ride—only a few still exist, most of them used by geishas when they go to their secret assignations in the cities' entertainment quarters.

When planning any kind of trip, try to avoid actually being in transit on any one of the major national holidays, for the Japanese themselves are indefatigable travellers. No park, shrine or mountain path is complete without its large groups of uniformed school-children or students, all equipped with cameras and in the charge of a leader who usually carries a flag of identification and talks incessantly.

Adults, similarly equipped and led, also travel frequently in package tour groups and the most painless way of seeing the main sights is undoubtedly to join them. Most are well organised and supplied with a guide who speaks at least some English. A wide variety of tours are available in and around every city and to various holiday resorts. They vary in duration from a few hours to a thirteen-day nationwide tour covering all the main centres of interest. There are also specially planned tours for those intent on skiing or mountaineering and 'industrial tours' round large factories and plants where Japanese specialties such as cameras or pearls are made. Details of these are available from the local tourist offices and from individual tour operators, most of them need to be booked in advance. Before paying, check that your fare includes such items as on-route meals, tips and admission fees which can add considerably to the cost otherwise.

A way of combining the pleasures of seeing the sights and the people without being herded around in a group the whole time is to go and stay at one of the many flourishing holiday resorts that have grown up at some of the most beautiful spots in the country — by the seashore, lakeside, mountain and hot spring. Many of the most outstanding scenic areas on the four main islands have now been designated as national parks — of which there are twenty-seven. There are also forty-seven quasi-national parks situated around landscaped features of particular appeal, such as headlands or woods. As in most countries where tourism is a highly developed industry, these places are equipped with facilities for enjoying such pursuits as skiing, boating and hiking and they are linked by coach to nearby towns. The National parks are also equipped with vacation villages set in natural scenery which provide simple lodgings and camp sites. Details of the parks, their location, extent and ways of reaching them are available from tourist offices.

The Japanese have a peculiar addiction for immersing themselves in very hot water, and for the past two thousand years have been bathing in the hot springs that exist in several regions — there are about a thousand in the country altogether. Hot-spring resorts, called *onsen*, are very Japanese affairs and the main purpose for visiting them is to soak for hours in the various waters, most of which are claimed to be of medicinal value. Many of these resorts are small, relatively quiet and off-the-beaten-track and they offer the foreign traveller a good opportunity for relaxation and enjoyment in a traditionally native manner — even if it may be difficult to adjust oneself to the temperatures of the actual waters, which can exceed 40 degrees centigrade. Short-stay coach tours operate to many of these little resorts and for details of those available in a particular region, ask at the local tourist office.

Staying and eating
In order to be sure of the accommodation you want, be sure to make bookings in advance; this is absolutely essential during the main tourist season, on national holidays and desirable at any time. Reservations can be made through agencies or by writing directly to hotels. In general, hotels, and inns fall into one of two categories — Japanese style or Western style, though a number try to combine the two. Hotels catering for Western tastes were a relative rarity until the 1950s and the most famous pre-war establishments situated in resorts such as Hakone and Karuizawa are redolent of the earlier, more exclusive era of the globetrotter and well worth a visit. Most of the recently built modern hotels are standard international in appearance, though often with

attractively orientalised interior design; they have modern facilities such as air-conditioning and central heating.

Nearly all towns of any size, especially in Honshu, will have at least one Western style hotel and there is a large selection to choose from in the cities and big holiday resorts. Most hostelries of good standard are members of the Japan Hotel Association and lists of addresses and prices are available from the tourist offices. The de-luxe and first-class establishments provide a standard of accommodation and service similar to that in the same class of international hotels the world over and they offer additional amenities such as currency exchanges, sauna baths, heated swimming pools and television in every room. The service is invariably obliging and efficient, but prices are high by most Western standards. Be warned that the rates quoted on arrival are only the basic and do not include breakfast or service charges, taxes and extras which can increase the eventual bill considerably. As a fixed service charge is levied, there is no need to tip individually—except porters. Resort hotels often have cheaper off-season, long-stay rates.

People travelling on limited budgets can make for the growing number of less expensive 'businessmen's hotels' that are often conveniently located near railway stations or city centres. They are quite clean (as Japanese hotels of all kinds are) and supplied with the basic mod-cons, but they have no room service, no large restaurants, cocktail lounges or the other 'luxury frills' that greatly add to the cost of more de-luxe establishments. There are also some quite adequate pensions in the cities, resorts and national parks—some of the last have Club Mediterranean type places with lodges and communal eating facilities.

Foreign travellers who have visions of taking off from the populated areas of the country with a rucksack perhaps and a little currency in search of out-of-the-way places should perhaps be warned that this is not such a simple matter as it is in much of Europe. Because such a high percentage of Japan is mountainous the majority of isolated, scarcely populated places are actually inhospitable and, as the Japanese have a very keen eye for the potential of any natural beauty spot, it is not easy to find areas of great charm that have not already been discovered by the ubiquitous groups of tourists.

It is certainly much cheaper to travel in remote rural areas, particularly if you can adapt to the local cuisines. The Japan National Tourist Organisation is recently trying to promote travel to the less popular resorts for those with limited means and it publishes lists of 'Reasonable Accommodations' in various parts of the country. It also produces a helpful guide to Budget Travel which suggests several practical ways of saving money on accommodation and food without actually having to rough it.

It is also good to know that Japan has the best youth hostel network in Asia, with about six hundred hostels throughout the country. Some of them are operated by the government, others are private and affiliated with Japanese Youth Hostels Inc. For the latter you need a membership card of your home country's youth hostel association or an international guest card. The hostels offer simple sleeping accommodation in dormitories, rented bedding, meals or self-cooking facilities and levy an extra charge for heating or air-conditioning. At some of the more remote resorts there are also Youth Travel Villages (Seishonen Ryoko-san) with camp sites, cabins and recreational facilities. Naturally, foreign visitors going to these kinds of youth-orientated establishments are expected to conform to Japanese styles of living and eating. For most of them there is no upper age limit, by the way.

An interesting recent development for the budget-minded traveller of any age who wants to get closer to the rice-roots of Japan than is usually possible on the conventional coach-and-hotel tour is to stay in a Minshuku, which is the nearest that one can easily get to being a paying guest in a Japanese family. Minshuku (there is no true English equivalent for the word) are usually run as a sideline by farmers, fishermen or other rurally based people or by Buddhist priests attached to temples. Their conditions and facilities vary considerably but most of them, especially the rural ones, provide the visitor with a chance to actually participate in the life of the local community. Guests are usually expected to share bedrooms and are offered two meals a day of the food normally eaten by the family and in a family setting. They are expected to bring their own towels, toiletries etc., make their own beds and generally offer a helping hand when required. JNTO publishes a list of accredited Minshuku which are located in most parts of the country. During peak travel months accommodation at them should be booked in advance.

If you feel that a Minshuku is rather beyond your Western capabilities of adaptation but still yearn for something more truly Japanese than the recently built international-style hotel, then visit a ryokan. Ryokan are very traditionally and distinctively Japanese and staying in at least one should be part of every foreign visitor's experience. Usually housed in low wooden buildings that look like superior private dwellings, they are immaculately clean, quiet and frequently surrounded by pleasantly landscaped gardens with ornamental ponds and groves of trees. Invariably, they are more expensive than the ordinary Western-style hotel, but the cost of breakfast and supper is customarily included in the overall price (midday meals must be ordered in advance). Native-style meals are brought to guests' rooms by a maid and there is not much choice of menu.

Guests are accommodated in a sitting room with an adjoining ante-room and, often, a verandah/sun room with chairs and tables. Most of the furnishings are in the simple and elegant native style however—sliding doors, tatami floors, cushions for sitting on and wall-hangings. At night the main room is converted to a comfortable bedroom in the old manner by the maid who spreads the thick futon on the floor, brings the bedding from a cupboard recess and lights a lamp. It is customary for guests to go and wash before supper (which is served early) in one large communal bathroom that is used by everyone; some ryokan have private bathrooms at extra cost these days. Wherever you bath, remember that it is not proper to wash youself with soap inside the tub. The correct procedure is to wash and rinse before a long soak in the hot water.

Correct ryokan etiquette also requires you to leave your outdoor footwear at the entrance-way where loose slippers are provided for walking about inside. The ultimate courtesy, in some establishments, is that your shoes will be polished and placed ready for you to wear on leaving. Ryokan also provide guests with ukata, the loose robes that are ideal for lounging about on the tatami in traditional fashion and even for sleeping in. Most ryokan have some form of central heating these days, but be warned that they can still be very chilly in winter. The Japan Ryokan Association provides a list of over two thousand ryokan that have been designated as 'meeting the requirements of foreign tourists'.

As with accommodation, so the food available in the country's restaurants can be roughly divided into Western or native style, but with a continuing and increasing trend to combine the two, or to 'Japanify' a particular Western dish. Naturally Japanese food (see chapter 2) is the principal fare in the ryokan, while Western-style hotels often serve both, and may well boast an international-type menu that includes such items as Italian spaghetti, Chinese chow-mien and American 'bif steak'.

There is more Western food of reasonable quality available in the cities than in the remoter provinces, but in most places you will find at least one café-restaurant serving such familiar items as hamburgers, fried chicken and sandwiches. Also, buffets and self-service restaurants can be found in many department stores; they usually serve both Japanese and Western food and offer an easy way of sampling one native delicacy at a time. Frequently, the business of selection is made easier by the plastic replicas of every dish that are on display at the restaurant entrance. Other good bargains are the 'tourist menus' offered by restaurants in cities and resorts; they consist of a three-course set meal in either Japanese or Western-style. Remember that, in high class restaurants, a ten percent tax is added to the bill.

Meals of various kinds, with drinks, are available in the night-clubs that have become increasingly popular in Japan during the past twenty years. The floorshows are invariably full of colour and zest and often put on with an amusing combination of Japanese and Western flair; for men, hostesses are available to sit and chat and serve as dancing partners if required. Such clubs are not for the budget-minded however, for prices of both food and drink are very high.

The Japanese Restaurant Association has a nationwide list of leading restaurants that cater specially for foreign tourists, though most of them tend to be on the expensive side. It is as well to remember that, with the exception of entertainment clubs, Japanese establishments serve the last meal of the day fairly early in the evening, so it is not easy to eat late at night. If you are hungry at such a time, try some delicious *yakatori* (chicken grilled on a skewer) that is sold at many open street stalls.

General tips for the tourist

Currency
The unit of currency is the yen. Coins come in denominations of 5, 10, 50 and 100; notes are a 100, 500, 1,000, 5000 and 10,000. To give a rough idea of monetary value: a ten yen piece will buy a postcard or a three-minute telephone call; hundred yens are needed for bus rides or vending machines; a single room in a Western-style hotel customarily costs between 1,500 and 5,500 yen for the basics.

Hygiene
The standard of public hygiene in Japan is high and the people
are extremely clean in their person, for everyone always takes a
daily bath. Sanitation facilities in the cities are usually Western
style, though very often there are 'oriental style' flush toilets.
Water is safe to drink and standards of food hygiene are excellent,
for the Japanese have something of a fetish about the freshness of
their food. Good hotels have facilities for laundering and dry-
cleaning and there are some coin-operated laundrettes in the main
cities.

Medical care
Generally, standards of medical care are high and hospitals have
all modern equipment. Many doctors and dentists speak at least
some English. There are hospitals and clinics in the major cities
that are registered with the International Association for Medical
Attention to Travellers. Make sure you have had the required
vaccinations before reaching the country, as health cards are
normally checked.

Communications
Domestic and foreign postal services in Japan are reliable and
efficient; telegrams sent in the Romanised alphabet, either
domestic or overseas, can be handed in at all large city telegraph
offices. Cities are excellently supplied with public telephones and
the automatic dial system is in widespread use, so one does not
have to struggle linguistically with an operator. Note that yellow
telephones are for long-distance out-of-city calls only.

Ninety-eight daily newspapers circulate in Japan; five of them
are in English of which the best known is *The Japan Times* which
has a long and distinguished journalistic history and is available
in all cities. Several periodicals of both general and specialist kind
are published in English and in all urban areas a variety of
international magazines and books in most European languages
are for sale. Radio Japan broadcasts regular news services in
English, while American and European films are sometimes shown
on television.

Shopping
Buying things is a major pursuit of the Japanese themselves and
their shops certainly offer countless temptations for the foreign
visitor. Certain articles that are listed in the Customs Regulations

issued on arrival can be purchased tax-free by foreigners who have
a 'Tax Exemption for Export' form which is attached to visitors'
passports, and obtainable at the store of purchase. Tax exemption
ranges from ten to forty percent, so it is certainly worth the effort
of acquiring. Among the most popular best bargains of the country
are cameras, transistor radios, cultured pearls, cloisonné ware,
ivories, prints, toys, silks, curios and lacquerware, Most of the
large shops are open from about 10 a.m. to 8 p.m. including
Sundays. The biggest department stores close one day a week,
usually Monday.

Dress
The Japanese tend to dress rather conventionally—men in neat
business suits, women in smart dresses and suits and students and
school-children usually wear uniforms. Only foreigners of small
stature can easily wear Japanese ready-made clothes and shoes;
but it is quite easy, and not very expensive, to get clothes made
to measure. Some stores stock large sizes for foreigners.

Meeting the people
It is not easy for the short-stay visitor to get to know any Japanese
well. It is not the native custom to invite strangers into the home
and there is no real equivalent of our habit of dropping in on
friends. Indeed, the Japanese themselves do not entertain in the
home very often and most visitors are family relatives. It is
therefore, especially difficult to meet an ordinary Japanese house-
wife, for example, for the man of the house usually takes his guests
to a restaurant and his wife seldom accompanies them. Similarly,
most bars and cafés will be filled with businessmen in the evenings
—the female sex being represented mainly by hostesses, students
and a few 'b.g's', which is the Japanese term for business girls.
Habits like these stem from the strict paternalism of the past, but
even the younger and more educated couples will be reluctant to
take foreigners home, partly because they feel that their living
standards are not up to those of the West.

If your time is limited therefore, the only quick way to circum-
vent these factors is to take advantage of the Home Visit Systems
that operate in eight major cities. These are organised by the Japan
Tourist Board and other travel agencies who furnish the names
and addresses of families willing to entertain foreigners on an
informal basis for a meal in their homes or a day's excursion. The
service is free, but it is usual to take presents to your hosts. If you

have a particular professional or technical skill, it may also be possible to meet people doing similar work through their particular associations. The tourist offices have lists of such professional associations and of groups such as Rotary and the Red Cross who welcome like-minded people from other countries.

6 AIDS FOR THE FOREIGN BUSINESSMAN

The historical and social background

To conduct business with the Japanese can be very pleasant and rewarding. Nevertheless it is as well to be prepared in advance for a certain number of situations, customs and attitudes that are usually unfamiliar to those whose previous experience has been confined to the business circles of Europe and America. To understand the reason for this, it is useful to know that modern Japanese codes of business behaviour do not stem from the same historical and social roots as those of Western nations whose current practices of national and international negotiation and agreement evolved during the eighteenth and nineteenth centuries as a result of the dramatic impact of the Industrial Revolution.

In Japan however, during the long period of seclusion under the shogunate, merchants and traders of all types were a generally despised class with little status in the community, few political rights and little ambition beyond the accumulation of more wealth which they could only spend in fairly restricted ways. This situation was the result of the government's deliberate policy of suppressing all kinds of enterprise and individual entreprenurial activity in order to maintain the stable feudal, agrarian foundations of the state.

Following the Meiji revolution of 1868 when sweeping reforms took place in all areas of Japanese life, these restrictions were abolished; merchants were allowed much more freedom to trade internally and, for the first time for nearly three hundred years, were actually encouraged to establish foreign commercial connections. Under the shogunate, people of all classes were more or less obliged to follow the occupations of their forefathers; these regulations too were abolished which meant that enterprising new blood was brought into the merchant class. It was at this period that a few members of the well-born, disciplined and still much respected samurai class first set up as entrepreneurs and, significantly, they were called 'gentlemen-businessmen' to distinguish them from the ordinary lowly born merchants.

The aim of these men was officially expressed as 'service to the nation through industry'. This sense of public obligations as well as private profit still survives today, incidentally, for modern leaders of industry place great stress on the community and welfare aspects of their work and their responsibilities for furthering the cultural life of the nation. Witnesss to this, are, for example, the numbers of small art collections maintained by firms for the enjoyment of their employees and/or the general public and the elegance of the public foyers and reception rooms in business organisations that are lavishly designed to give pleasure to all who go there. On the other hand, the dominant ideas of the leaders of industry during the Meiji era were essentially paternalistic and oligarchical rather than democratic, and these traits too are still apparent to some extent today.

Owing to the speed and efficacy of Japan's adoption of the economic ideas and modern technologies of the Western world, the country had created a fairly strong industrial base by the time that World War I began, though the emphasis was on light industry, especially textiles. During the war however, Japan made great strides in both its light and heavy industrial growth, its export trade boomed and, for the first time in its history, the country could boast of a huge export surplus. As a result of these successes, profits soared and the occupation of businessmen at last became a thoroughly honourable one, open to all men who possessed sufficient drive and dedication. The majority of top businessmen still came from the urban middle classes however and during the period between the two world wars, this section of Japanese society became more politically active and vocal than it had ever been before. It exerted considerable pressure towards the liberalising of the earlier feudal structures of the big business world. The general national movement towards a more open and democratic style of government received a setback however during the mid-1930s when the military became so powerful.

Throughout the first part of the twentieth century therefore the prevailing commercial climate in Japan was conservative compared to the standards of the contemporary West. And ordinary people who were generally unaccustomed to the rights and risks of a free-enterprise economy tended to shy away from individual entrepreneurism and commercial innovations. It was at this time that a great deal of economic control became concentrated in the hands of a few enormous combines who attained the monopoly of power in a wide variety of fields such as banking, insurance, shipping, manufacturing and overseas investment. The power of these combines continues to this day and they dominate whole sections of the Japanese economy. While these combines have usually had the effect of improving the country's technological development and encouraging the accumulation of capital for investment, they have also tended to perpetuate the traditions of hierarchical control.

However, the term 'hierarchical control' may only be a rather loaded Western interpretation of the situation for, in the Japanese view, employer-employee commitments have always been defined in terms of human relationships rather than as authoritarian contractual agreements imposed by above. Rather like a traditional marriage, an employee is expected to join the 'family' of a company and stay there until he retires — usually at fifty-five, though there is currently pressure to raise the retirement age and make it more flexible.

The benefits of this so-called 'lifetime employment' system from the workers' point of view are that, in reward for long and continuous service, they receive generous retirement and welfare allowances, annual bonuses and various fringe benefits such as educational and recreational facilities, financial help with medical insurance and housing and, in some cases, child-care facilities and the chance to shop at discount stores. Moreover, it is very unusual for a company to sack an employee and so his future is secure. An employee's status within the firm is based on the seniority system which fixes wages and levels of almost automatic promotion as the years go by — and this can lead to a high executive level.

From the employers' point of view, these pyramid-shaped, closely knit systems of business organisation develop a high sense of participation among employees who identify closely with the fortunes of the organisation to which they give so much. As a result, relationships within the business structure often tend to be tense under the surface just because they are so unrelieved. Such a system has distinct advantages of course, but it does hamper the flexibility of labour and restrict workers' horizons because they are usually trained strictly in accordance with the needs and prospects of one particular firm so, as the years go by, their opportunities for change or for any individual initiative are thus greatly narrowed.

The existence of these large business combines allied to the Japanese people's willingness and ability to work hard and unquestioningly while living frugally and peacably did much to

1 The Great Buddha (Diabutsu) at Kamakura

2 The Ginza, Tokyo – one of the liveliest shopping-streets in the world

3 The Akasaka district of Tokyo, a typical city-scape

4 The Karamon Gate, one of several highly ornamented entrances at the
Toshugu shrine, Nikko
5 A bowman on guard; this colourful, realistic figure is typical of many to
be seen at Nikko's Toshugu shrine

6 This splendid, cryptomeria-lined avenue leading to Nikko's Toshugu shrine is well trodden by tourists throughout the year

7 The classical Noh stage, with masked performers, musicians and chorus

8 A traditionally dressed geisha, seated on tatami, is the hostess at a tea-ceremony

9 This view of Mount Fuji, taken from Mount Tenjo, shows the sacred mountain at its peerless best

10 The five-storeyed donjon of Osaka Castle, beautifully reconstructed in
the original style of castle strongholds

11 The Ginkakuji, Kyoto's gracious Silver Pavilion, set in a landscaped garden

12 The main entrance to Tofukuji temple, one of Kyoto's many historical
religious buildings

13 The massive Todaiji temple at Nara houses the great bronze Buddha
that was cast in the eighth century

14 Japan's best-known five-storeyed pagoda – in the grounds of the Horyuji temple at Nara

15 One of the powerful guardians of the eighth-century Chumon Gate at the Horyuji temple in Nara

16 A small pavilion in the grounds of the Katsura Imperial Villa, Kyoto,
considered the ultimate in Japanese landscape gardens

17 An early-morning street scene in one of the older quarters of Kyoto

18 The entrance to a long-established ryokan (inn) in Kyoto

19 Drying rice on racks at a farm near Izumo

20 A street scene in Kurashiki, a town famous for its canals and unusual museums
21 A Buddhist priest rakes the sand of a temple 'flat garden'

22 Beneath these rafts at Kashikojima hang wire cages full of pearl-bearing oysters

produce the 'miracle' of the country's spectacular economic recovery during the post-war period. And, since the mid-1970s when Japan's boom was at its peak, there has been increasing pressure on major companies to invest overseas and develop export opportunities, particularly in Australia and the less developed parts of south Asia. The government is encouraging this process, but most of the impetus is coming from the rapid growth of the big corporations themselves together with the development of modern products that are proving attractive to foreign markets.

In line with the increased prosperity of recent years, labour unions in Japan have become more vocal in their claims on behalf of workers and labour relations are a growing concern among managements. Only a few Japanese unions are based on one industry or craft as in the West, rather they are 'enterprise unions' formed on an enterprise-by-enterprise or workshop-by-workshop basis. This results in the existence of a very large number of unions — about 70,000 in all and with a small average membership. Many of them form labour federations by industry or type of enterprise and these federations are members of national labour organisations, the most powerful of which being the General Council of Trade Unions of Japan (Sohyo).

Union workers in general are more critical than formerly about delays in improving their immediate environments and more concerned about health hazards caused by various kinds of industrial occupation. Their increasing knowledge of the rest of the world has made them more aware that their housing standards in particular are still low compared to those of many other developed countries. Another new factor for Japanese management to consider is the appearance on the scene of a modern type of highly skilled 'salary man', usually a professional or technical expert, who refuses to fit into the traditions of the life-employment system and moves from one firm to another in search of rapid promotion and higher wages in a manner that was almost unthinkable twenty years ago.

The greater prosperity and promises of more individual mobility that are characteristic of the younger Japanese generation mean that even average white-collar workers are more cosmopolitan in their outlook and have more direct experience of other countries than used to be the case. Nowadays, a considerable number of Japanese actually live and work abroad for years at a stretch in the service of their self-proclaimed 'multi-national' companies. But two significant factors have emerged from this development. One is that Japanese firms operating abroad remain generally reluctant to change their own policies and practices in any way to accord with those of the host country; the second is that the experience of the overseas 'tour of duty' is not necessarily considered a feather in the businessman's cap as it usually is in the West. Rather the reverse, for the man and his whole family are expected to 'rehabilitate' themselves carefully and thoroughly into their normal and proper way of life when they return home.

As these points suggest, the veneer of 'internationalisation' is quite a recent acquisition of the Japanese and it is usually only skin-deep, which it is as well to remember when you are dealing with even the well-travelled. It is also worth considering that the new form of Japanese internationalisation (unlike the earlier Meiji version) does not always signify the indiscriminate adoption of European ideas or business methods. As Japanese theorists take pains to point out to Westerners these days, international companies of today do not necessarily have to accept uncondition-ally the rules for economic exchange that were originally worked out by and for the benefit of Western countries. Similarly, rapid social and technological development does not lead inevitably towards American-style capitalism.

Preparation and practice

To oil the wheels of commercial negotiation and increase mutual understanding between you and your Japanese hosts in the business world it is as well to bear the following points in mind. Firstly, because of the structure of Japan's business organisations, employees are acutely aware of titles and positions of relative seniority and it is advisable to know how they relate to each other within their hierarchy and what protocol is due to what position. Secondly, and because the people do not like to be taken by surprise in their business dealings, for this can cause embarrass-ment, they like plenty of warning of a visitor's arrival. This gives them time to assess the exact status of the visitor and to arrange meetings of both a formal and informal nature that are then considered appropriate. In short, nothing should be too hurried or left to chance—the unexpected caller who drops in during a twenty-four hour stop-over between Sydney and San Francisco wanting to negotiate an important contract is not popular.

Be sure to take as many business introductions with you as possible. The Japanese themselves use introductions a great deal in both their business and social life as part of their mutual-help group networks. So, if you can claim past contacts with a firm and/or knowledge of other company-men this is helpful, for it takes some time to break the ice initially and build up a feeling of confidence and trust. Once such a relationship is established, however, it will generally be maintained and indeed strengthened over a long period.

To facilitate initial meetings, be sure to take plentiful supplies of your own business name card (with full title and position printed in both Japanese and English). At all business and social functions these cards are exchanged freely and this should be done with a certain degree of ceremony and attention, allowing time for an exchange of pleasantries and a mutual registering of identity and status. Japan Air Lines can provide name cards of the correct type for all their passengers on request and at a reasonable charge provided sufficient notice is given.

It is also useful to know that Japan Air Lines runs an 'Executive Service' for businessmen which can provide spacious accommodation in twenty-one luxury hotels throughout the East at fairly short notice for all its individual passengers. There is also a JAL executive lounge in the Imperial Hotel in Tokyo which is equipped with office aids and personnel to answer queries. Some other hotels too offer facilities for the short-term hiring of stenographers, interpreters, electric typewriters etc. For those with specific marketing interests, Japan Air Lines has set up a business information service that provides official statistics, details of market trends, addresses of commercial firms and so on.

To attract more visitors to their country the Japanese have, for several years now, encouraged the holding of large international and business conventions in their major cities. More than two hundred large international conventions per year are now held there and in 1977 a total of more than 24,000 delegates attended. Their conference halls and adjoining facilities are purpose-built and of good modern design—the International Conference Hall at Kyoto is particularly outstanding. These conference centres are equipped with secretarial and interpreter services and conference programmes invariably include some sightseeing tours and additional programmes for 'the accompanying spouses' of delegates. For details of the halls, and accommodation available contact the Japanese Convention Bureau which is part of the national tourist organisation.

By present-day Western standards the Japanese behave rather

formally during their conventions and business meetings. Mostly the seating in reception and conference rooms is allotted with strict regard to rank and seniority and visitors are usually accompanied ('marked' it has been unkindly suggested) by a Japanese of equivalent rank to themselves. Great respect is always paid to the opinions of the superior in the room and it is sometimes hard to initiate discussion on delicate issues especially with those of subordinate rank. The Japanese have a natural tendency to shy away from direct confrontation and decision-making—as the first Western diplomats to the country discovered. When matters became too thorny the Japanese ministers were liable to disappear for days on end suffering from what was called 'official sickness'. Once a contract is agreed upon however, the Japanese will be a hundred percent behind it, but (and there is always a 'but') if conditions change or deteriorate, they will soon demand 're-negotiations'.

The lavishness of the Japanese businessman's expense account has become legendary in international circles during the past ten years. But the scene has changed recently owing to the current comparative recession which has caused widespread alarm and has led to a general cut-back in luxury expenditure. Now only those at highest executive level can expect to enjoy the really extra-lavish 'night on the town' that was quite customary a few years ago. Nevertheless it is still considered more or less mandatory and polite to attend at least one dinner function with the colleagues you have met during the day. This is usually held at a restaurant, a club or one of the new noisy and trendy 'night-spots'.

The ultimate compliment for the foreign businessman is still to be invited to a traditional geisha house where the atmosphere is thoroughly and delightfully Japanese. Dinners in all these establishments usually begin early, for the leisurely, almost ritual-istic consumption of many courses of food is considered the event of the evening—which usually ends fairly early too. On such occasions the Japanese relax quite readily and it is considered a compliment to the foreign guests if, for example, the president of the company eventually takes off his jacket and tells a few jokes. The ability to sing a little, do a card trick or two is also much appreciated. It is also much appreciated that when dining at a geisha house, foreigners join in the simple forfeit games with good humour and manifest appropriate enthusiasm for the pleasant garden surroundings and the performance of singing and dancing provided by the female entertainers of the establishment.

It is very rare for the wives of Japanese businessmen to be invited to any of these business-oriented functions and this makes it difficult for a Westerner who has his own wife with him. It is unfortunately even more difficult for a foreign woman who is negotiating business in her own right to be taken seriously. The Japanese are not yet really accustomed to dealing with women as equals in positions of authority and responsibility; they simply have not evolved the correct linguistic usages or the appropriate behaviour to deal with such contingencies. This situation will undoubtedly improve in the future as more foreign women and more Japanese women also attain high-ranking positions, but for the present it is as well that women going there on business be aware of, though not deterred by, this fact.

If you are invited to a businessman's home to meet his family or to a performance of some traditional entertainment such as Kubuki, then these are real compliments. For the Japanese do not readily admit strangers into their private domains and they are quick to discern if your appreciation of them is genuine. If you are so invited, it is considered polite to take a small present, and indeed there are several occasions when it is useful to have a supply of small gifts from your own native country, for the Japanese frequently press theirs upon you and are always very generous with their hospitality.

7 TOKYO: MEGALOPOLIS OF THE EAST

Tokyo is an acquired taste and to acquire it one needs a penchant for the urban-oriental. The city is a prime example of the genre, the largest megalopolis in the whole of the East, covering 2000 square kilometres and with a population exceeding nine million. Moreover the density of this population is so high that, of the total households, one quarter live in apartments with an average of 1.2 rooms per household. These crammed households sprawl over the horizons of the flat Kanto plain, an uneasy agglomeration of flimsy, dun-coloured, low-roofed dwellings and concrete blocks of flats, their strange proximity broken only by the wide swathes of expressways, rail and subway lines and the networks of narrow secretive alleys.

The city's conspicuous lack of the picturesque and quaint (especially at first sight—there *are* such sights to be found) is usually rather a shock to those whose images of Japan are coloured by the traditional, rurally inspired pictures of cherry trees in blossom, mist-wreathed mountains, thatched villages nestling beside peaceful streams. But this city is the epitome of modern post-war Japan—wealthy, restless, youthful, pushy, trendy, dedicated to the present and future, not to the past. The most typical figures on its streets are nattily suited businessmen carrying briefcases, earnest-looking, black-uniformed students of engineering or science, secretaries and typists (called 'b.g's' meaning 'business-girls') wearing the latest fashions, looking very assured and sophisticated.

Human settlement around the Gulf of Edo is recorded from the twelfth century onwards, and it first rose to fame in the middle of the fifteenth century when one of the leading clans built a fortress there. But the real period of the city's splendour began in 1590, when Ieyasu Tokugawa made it his provincial capital. Thirteen years later, when he became Shogun, thousands of his retainers settled round their lord in the capital and all the daimyo, the territorial nobles, were obliged to keep their families there, as hostages to their loyalty.

During the long period of the shogunate, Edo was divided into districts for security reasons, each with its own internal regulations and officers to enforce them. The borders of each district were unmistakeably defined by guarded stockades erected at intervals along the main thoroughfares, and even today, though the stockades have long since vanished, many of the districts are recognisable entities—not necessarily in socio-economic terms, but because they differ in general character and function from their neighbours.

When the shogunate was overthrown in 1868, the new Emperor Meiji chose Edo, renamed Tokyo, the Eastern Capital, for his imperial capital and decided to reside there rather than in Kyoto, the historical imperial seat. From then on and up to the present day, the country's political, administrative, financial and legislative affairs have been headquartered in the city; it is where the most powerful men in the land live and to which all the provincial young hopefuls aspire.

This continuing concentration of authority within one already over-populated area has exacerbated Tokyo's chronic problems of congestion and urban pollution. The River Sumida, along the green banks of which the city's first fortress was built, is now a murky, heavily polluted waterway that laps the walls of factories and warehouses. Mount Fuji, whose symmetrical, usually snow-capped cone was, in the olden days, an ever-visible symbol to Tokyo's citizens of their proud nationhood, is now seldom visible —except on public holidays when the factories close and the air is temporarily freed from their obscuring emissions. Air pollution, which sometimes rises to positively dangerous levels, is just one of Tokyo's present troubles; its citizens also suffer excessive traffic noise, summer water shortages and inadequate sewage services in some districts. However, such ills are common to most of the world's big cities, especially those which have expanded so fast in the past thirty years, and so they should come as no great surprise to visitors from the West.

Similarly, the main streets of the city will seem only too familiar, for many of them, in the Maranouchi district and the main Chuo Ward, are lined with office blocks housing the headquarters of major banks, shipping companies and business firms. The architecture of central Tokyo is so undistinguished partly because the city was almost totally destroyed twice in the past sixty years—by the dreadful earthquake of 1923 and by the Allied bombing holocaust at the end of World War II. In earlier centuries, nearly all the buildings were wooden (amazingly, about three quarters of them still are, by pure roof-count) and thus the city has always been very vulnerable to destruction by earthquake, fire and typhoon. The consequences of this catastrophe-ridden past is that one cannot, as in Paris, London or Delhi, say, get the best out of Tokyo by working through a list of long-established historical, religious and cultural 'sights' and ancient monuments. It has in fact many charms and many fascinating aspects which depend very much on one's ability to enjoy the varied spectacle of thoroughly urban, thoroughly oriental life. This means that the city's attractions are not easy to categorise, they are often side-street, casual, unassuming, partaking more of the still-transient present than the hallowed past, and most foreign visitors to Tokyo gain as much pleasure from going to its numerous department stores, cafés, exhibitions, galleries and parks as from the contemplation of its historical monuments.

For one thing there is no excuse for feeling boredom in Tokyo because there is an ever-changing multiplicity of things to do and see. An easy way of finding out what's on is to ring the Teletourist Service which gives comprehensive taped information on current happenings, and to buy the weekly newspaper, *The Tour Companion* which is written in English and gives details of such attractions as restaurants, shopping specialities, transport, special events, exhibitions and even sauna and massage parlours—which, according to connoisseurs are some of the best in the world. To suggest the diverse flavour of the city, a recent edition was advertising six performances of Noh theatre, flamenco dancing, special movies and cheap movies, burlesque shows, a classic puppet drama at the National Theatre and the seasonal programme of Kabuki at the Kabuki-za; no less than thirty-five musical events ranging from piano soloists, through samisen recitals, jazz quartets, demonstrations of drum beating, classical court music and a concert given by the Leningrad State Philarmonic Orchestra. Exhibitions sprout like overnight mushrooms encouraged by the people's indefatigable enthusiasm for the visually beautiful in all its aspects. So, during one week in Tokyo it is possible to see, for instance, displays of woodblock prints, T'ang dynasty pottery, old tea utensils, Noh masks, kasuri cloth with splashed-pattern designs, World War II photographs, ancient Chinese mirrors and bronzes, Persian manuscripts, handmade kites from south Asia, mother-of-pearl inlay from Taiwan, modern oil paintings and, of course, the seasonal flower arrangements.

Many of these exhibitions and recitals are small-scale, held in various hotels, department stores, out-of-the-way halls and the top floors of skyscraper office blocks—which all adds to the fun.

The newspaper also publishes lists of restaurants recommended for visitors and here again the choice is practically limitless, varying from the Tokyo branch of Maxims through Brazilian, Russian, Indonesian, Korean to plain old English pub fare. The many Western-style hotels in the first-class and de-luxe range are rather 'in' places to meet these days. They have comfortable restaurants and bars with international-type names such as Starlit Lounge and Orchid Bar, many of them on top storeys with spectacular urban views, especially at night. At the other end of the price scale, there are dozens of hamburger, pizza and fried chicken bars and there are also moderately priced self-service restaurants in many of the large office buildings which are frequented at lunch-time by office workers but are also open to the general public. The Japanese have also adopted the Germanic idea of the 'cheap and cheerful' beer halls and gardens. The roofs of several large department stores are converted into beer gardens during the summer and it is both pleasant and economical to sit quaffing mugs of the best local brews—among them Kirin, Asahi and Sapporo, the famous beer of Hokkaido. Other places where one can happily linger over a drink are the so-called 'jazz tea-shops' each one of which specialises in a particular kind of musical entertainment.

The range of tours that one can take in and around Tokyo is also very wide, with long, one-day excursions to all the major sights in the surrounding area. There are also special interest tours—to parks, out-of-town exhibitions and to Zen temples for one-day meditation sessions. Night-tours of the city include visits to barbecue-dining gardens, night-clubs, music halls and 'geisha parties'—the last, incidentally, are entirely tourist-oriented and should not be mistaken for the real traditional thing.

However, it is time to take a look at the city's past. In its very centre stands the Imperial Palace encircled by inner moats and high stone walls which border on the Maranouchi business district. The palace itself is built on the site of Edo Castle that was founded in the fifteenth century and was the residence of the Tokugawa Shoguns for 265 years. Part of the Imperial Palace buildings were destroyed in World War II and the new design in ferro-concrete and Japanese style, dates from 1968. The building is partly opened to the public twice a year—at the New Year when thousands of citizens come to pray and celebrate, and on the Emperor's birthday, which is 29 April. In front of the Palace's main entrance there is an attractive plaza adorned with lawns and clumps of pines which is a popular meeting place; to the east is a lovely traditional Japanese landscape garden which is open to the public for a few hours on five days a week.

The palace is the symbol of the nation's unity and its long imperial history; but the real power is concentrated in the National Diet Building that stands on Kasimigaseki Hill. It is an imposing concrete and granite structure dominated by a high tower which was completed in 1936 and bears all the marks of early twentieth century public architecture, being both grandiose and solid. Inside it is more attractive, with marble floors, galleries and wood-panelling—admission to the Visitors' Gallery may be obtained while the Diet is in session. North of the building is the National Diet Library which contains about two and a half million books. Bibliophiles interested in the history of the East, incidentally, should make a special excursion to one of the main library's branches, the Tokyo Bunko, or Oriental Library. Based on a collection of the late Dr George Morrison, it contains some splendid material on Asian subjects and some rare early books about the development of Japan as seen through Western eyes.

South of the palace and the solid governmental and administrative buildings is Yurakucho, the central entertainment district. It is a lively conglomeration of theatres, bars, movie-houses and restaurants. The famous Nichigeki and Takarazuka variety theatres are here, and they present a series of large, lavish song-and-dance spectaculars in which literally hundreds of chorus girls participate—seemingly with great gusto. The footwork is not always impeccable and the music is a very loud East-West blend, but the stunning variety and colour of the sets and the stage-effects are most enjoyable. The best times of all to go are for the spring or autumn shows when the stages are awash with plastic pink cherry blossoms or falling yellow leaves.

This is also a good district for exploring the bars and coffee shops that are done up in every conceivable kind of décor and serving music of every conceivable sort along with drinks and snacks. Here also are numerous pachinko parlours, for pachinko is the national pin-ball game. Habitués play it for hours on end and occasionally win tiny prizes; the clink of the silver pachinko ball is now a familiar note in every city.

Yurakucho borders on the Chuo Ward and the broad road that

extends through it is the busiest in the capital. At one end is the famous landmark of the Nihonbashi bridge, which is considered the centre not only of the city but of the whole empire and the place from which all distances in the country are measured. The bridge has been rebuilt several times since its original construction in 1603. 'At present', says the official guide to the city, with unusually expressed distaste, '...an elevated expressway runs low over the bridge and disfigures its fine contours'.

The busiest section of the road is the Ginza, one of the most glittering, lively and fascinating thoroughfares in the entire orient. The best-known department stores are located here, such as Matsuya, Mitsukoshi and Matsuzakaya, as well as a parade of specialist stores selling curios, cultured pearls, watches and jewellery. Japanese department stores are like no others and deserve a few hours of any visitor's time—even those with little money or inclination to buy.

They house art, craft and flower-arranging exhibitions, tea-ceremony pavilions as well as the more usual displays of furniture, electrical, musical and camera equipment, tastefully arranged displays of china and pottery. There are large sections devoted to the selling of silks and brocades and elegant kimonos, with all their traditional accessories; in other sections you can see genuine antiques, screens, scrolls and some extremely rare and expensive objets d'art; others yet are devoted to the display of toys, models and decorations used during the various national festivals. (If you can't decide what to buy from such a plethora, go to the top floor of Daimaru department store where there are showcases containing the arts, handicrafts and textiles that are specialities of each region.)

The basement of most stores are food halls, featuring a lot of curiously coloured, wispy, raw and dried looking items that only a few foreigners recognise, and on the roofs there are gardens with outdoor cafés, pet stores and playgrounds for the children. It is no wonder that many Japanese make their nearest large department store the object of a whole day's family excursion.

Just east of the Ginza is the Kabukiza theatre, where plays are staged throughout the year. Rebuilt in 1950, it's an impressive example of modern Japanese architecture; it seats up to 2,600 people and during the long intervals in the performances, the audience patronises the booths selling souvenirs and sweetmeats, and the restaurants and tea-bars that are all contained within the building.

Apart from the city's central hub, there are a number of outlying quarters that are well worth visiting. The most easily accessible is Asakusa, one of the oldest districts which, with its many covered passageways, suggests the strange mysteries of an oriental bazaar. The open shop fronts are gaudily decorated with plastic flowers and lanterns; there are burlesque shows, food-stalls, tea houses and the Kannon Temple, the approach to which is lined with souvenir shops selling tiny Buddhas, lucky charms and all manner of toys. Altogether Asakusa has an air of jolly, slightly vulgar bustle created by the thousands of ordinary folk who have gone there over the years to enjoy themselves.

Two other shopping areas that are the pride of modern Tokyoites are Shibuya and Shinjuku, which are both large enough to seem like separate towns. There are plazas for strolling and sitting out, branches of all the major department stores, and small shops of every conceivable kind. Of the two, Shibuya is the more expensive and more of its clientele live in the middle-class apartment blocks nearby; Shinjuku has long enjoyed a rather rakish reputation and is at its off-beat best in the evenings, when a glittering array of neon lights sparkle from its many caberets and clubs. Music belts out from all directions and from nowhere more loudly than the huge Koma stadium which stages a diverse programme of musical events throughout the year. It is exciting to visit the crowded little bars and neon-lit clubs late at night – but be careful, for the area has a bad reputation for clip joints and mugging.

Some of the country's highest rise buildings have been erected during the 1970s to the west of Shinjuku station – which itself demands superlatives for it handles more than a million passengers a day. The Summoto Building with linked underground shopping centres, houses the offices of more than fifty companies and about seven thousand people work within its concrete walls, so that it is almost like a small town. The Mitsui Building, built in 1974, has fifty-five storeys and is the highest in the country.

Being the ultra-modern city that it is, you should not expect to find very many noted ancient buildings in Tokyo; moreover many of the proud mansions and large temples of the Togukawa days have been destroyed by fire, earthquake and war. One temple remarkable for its historical associations of that earlier period, however, is the Sengakuji, south-West of Shiba Park which is the burial place of the Forty-Seven Ronin. These men were samurai and their lord, Asona of Ako, was ordered to commit suicide in 1701 for having been provoked by another lord, called Kira, to draw his sword in the reigning Shogun's palace. Resolving to revenge their master's death in faithful samurai fashion, the men became ronin (that is 'masterless samurai') and the following year they besieged Lord Kira's residence in Edo and eventually slew him. Having completed their revenge, they reported the deed to the authorities and were ordered to commit mass suicide by dis-embowellment—this they did near the site of the Sengakuji. Their graves are in the court at the side and their relics and wooden images are in the temple museum. This tale of the Forty-Seven Ronin's loyalty and deed of revenge is known to all Japanese; it was dramatised under the title of Chusingura and is still a popular classic on the Kabuki stage.

Another important monumental building to see in Tokyo is the beautiful Meiji shrine, to which thousands of patriotic citizens make pilgrimage every year from all parts of the country. First built in 1920, the shrine is dedicated to the Emperor Meiji who did so much to open up and modernise Japan and who is still greatly revered for this. The shrine itself is of Shintoistic simplicity and beauty and behind it is a treasure house containing many mementos and relics of the dynamic Meiji era, including the carriage in which the Emperor rode when the first imperial constitution was promulgated in 1889.

The Inner Garden of the shrine is thickly wooded and has a beautiful lake and a famous iris garden, with more than a hundred varieties of the flower, which is at its best in May. On days of national festival, especially on 3 November which is the anniversary of the Emperor's birthday, displays of ancient court dancing and music are given on the stage in front of the garden's main building.

The Outer Garden, which has only been developed in the last fifteen years or so, boasts an attractively designed memorial picture-gallery with pictures of Meiji Japan in both Western and Japanese styles. A number of large sporting facilities are also here, including the National Stadium built for the 1964 Olympic Games, stadiums for baseball, rugby football and a vast indoor swimming pool. Not far from the Meiji Outer Garden is the Shinjuku Gyoen National Garden with large glasshouses containing brilliant displays of tropical and sub-tropical plants. It is also a favourite spot with Tokyoites for viewing the spring cherry-blossom, and splendid shows of chrysanthemums are held there every autumn.

The majority of the capital's best museums and galleries are conveniently clustered together at Ueno Park, north of the centre and on direct underground and bus lines. The principal National Museum building houses about 86,000 exhibits showing the history, arts and folklore of Japan itself with many others of Chinese, Korean and Indian origin; among them are several pieces that have been designated as National Treasures or Important Cultural Properties. The richness and variety of the collection has to be seen to be believed; but look out especially for the quaint stone Haniwa figurines dating from the fifth century; the grimacing demon or god masks used in the seventh century for the performance of Gagaku court-dances; and the decorative costumes worn by the nobility of the early Heian.

Just behind the main museum is a lovely traditional garden with ponds and old wooden pavilions. Nearby is the Metropolitan Fine Art Gallery which holds special nationally renowned exhibitions of art and calligraphy throughout the year. There is also the Museum of Modern Art that houses the Matsukata collection that includes works by many celebrated European sculptors and artists such as Cezanne, Degas, Monet and Rodin.

At the end of an avenue of cherry trees stands the imposing Toshugu shrine, national treasure dedicated to the memory of the powerful Tokugawa Ieyasu; it is made up of several elaborately decorated buildings and the approach to them is past rows of stone and bronze lanterns. Other smaller museums within the Ueno complex specialise in displays of ancient swords and armour and, in modern craft objects and in recent developments of science and technology. The Bunka Concert Hall is world-famed for its excellent acoustics and in the nearby zoological garden you'll find lots of unusual animal and bird species and an excellently stocked aquarium. All in all, and whatever your interests, it is worth spending several hours at Ueno, even if your time in the capital is limited.

In addition to the particularly outstanding buildings, monuments, museums and tempting shops that are common to most modern capital cities, Tokyo boasts one or two surprises. There is, for example, Tokyo Tower, the proud structure in the large, well-laid-out Shiba Park which, as the Japanese never tire of pointing out, is higher than the Eiffel Tower of Paris. It is adorned with two observation platforms that offer stunning bird's-eye views of the entire city (and, sometimes its smoke-laden atmosphere).

Enthusiasts of Japanese gardening should make for the

Korakuen and Rikugien, two of the most famous gardens in the country and beautifully representative of the traditional land-scaping of former days. Both are within easy reach of the centre by bus or underground, though happily secluded from its usual hubbub. Lovers of ships and seas (which the Japanese certainly are) should also visit the Museum of Maritime Science in Koto Ward that was opened in 1974. It is a six-storey concrete structure shaped most imaginatively like a passenger ship and it is filled with comprehensive exhibitions of marine history and displays relating to the future potential of the oceans.

There are three other very distinctively Japanes museums that are worth making special trips to see. The first is the Paper Museum in which every exhibit is made of that fragile substance and all beautifully; the Museum of Sumo which tells the full story of the arts and personalities of Japanese wrestlers; and there is the Nippon Minka-en, a very unusual and refreshing outdoor exhibition in which the traditional Japanese dwelling-houses, stores and stables have been carefully reconstructed to conjure the atmosphere of the ordinary rural Japan of the past.

Lastly, and for a look at the ordinary everyday scenes of the present, it is worth getting up quite early and going to the Tsukiji, the enormous wholesale fish-market. For most of the morning this scaly emporium is a smelly and colourful bustle where fish merchants, fishermen and the city's thousands of restauranteurs meet to bargain over catches that may include everything from oysters to sharks. If you had any doubt that the Japanes love to eat a great deal of fish, this is the place to go. And it is also the place to try some of the recently caught fish for yourself, served raw with cold rice and pickled vegetables in the traditional manner of sushi.

8 THE AREAS AROUND TOKYO

Yokohama

One of the most momentous of all East-West encounters took place in Yokohama in 1854 when Commodore Matthew Perry and his fleet of 'black ships' landed there to sign the Trading Treaty which Perry had presented to the Japanese the year before. At the time, Yokohama was just a fishing village of thatched huts beside a swamp, and the intrusion of so many 'red-haired barbarians' on the peaceful scene terrified the local inhabitants, for they had never clapped eyes on an occidental before. The Americans brought artifacts of the Western world to show the 'backward' Japanese: military instruments, a miniature locomotive that went round in a small circle and a telegraph. When the last was set up, people queued for hours to send each other messages.

Unable to resist this unwelcome and very forceful intrusion, the shogunate signed Perry's treaty and, in 1859, Yokohama became one of the first of the nation's five treaty ports in which foreigners were allowed to settle—though only within strictly defined limits and under restrictive conditions. By the 1860s, the former fishing village had become something of a boom town, with mercantile firms from China and Singapore setting up businesses, and there was a steady increase in trade with Europe and the United States. The paved Bund (waterfront) was soon lined with offices, warehouses and consulates, and the first wooden Western-style houses were built on the cliffs overlooking the sea, known as The Bluff. In 1872, the nation's first railway was opened linking Yokohama with the capital; that same year crowds gathered to watch the main streets in the native quarter lit up by gaslights. The first rickshaw was said to have been invented in Yokohama and the first cricket game on Japanese soil to have been played behind the Bund.

By the last years of the century, Yokohama had become a flourishing centre for internation trade between the United States and China and a very popular port of call for ocean liners carrying 'globetrotters' on their Eastern tours. By then the character of the place was firmly established—solidly, but not too flashily prosperous; comfortable, secure and cosmopolitan; boasting a number of dignified buildings and dwellings in the oriental-colonial style; containing a number of energetic and committed foreign residents who worked hard, ate and drank hard and played hard in the customary colonial fashion. In 1923 the greater part of the port was flattened by the same earthquake that destroyed much of Tokyo; at the end of World War II, Yokohama, like Tokyo, was again flattened by air-raids.

Undaunted, Yokohama has now risen for the third time and today it is the largest port and third largest city in the country, with an estimated population of two and a half million. As a result of this tremendous expansion of both Tokyo and Yokohama there is scarcely a green space left between them. Thousands commute daily between the two cities, and both are similarly afflicted with problems of congestion and pollution.

To glean an idea of how Yokohama used to be in the not-very-distant past, visit first the international Cemetery at Yamatemachi on The Bluff which is still the best residential area. It contains many interesting monuments of foreigners, written in many languages—merchants, travellers, artists, missionaries, sailors and consuls who all loved the quiet life of the old oriental port.

Below The Bluff is Motomachi, a well-known shopping street with boutiques selling a tempting variety of curios, clothes, jewellery and craftwork; because of the long-established foreign connection, its shopkeepers are more than usually fluent in English. Yokohama also has an excellent Chinatown, with many clean, unpretentious restaurants selling Chinese food cooked by Chinese and the dignified Grand Hotel on the waterfront is redolent of a generation ago—when cargos came off ships as cargos instead of stacks of featureless containers. A short ride from the centre of the city takes you to the Sankeien Gardens, with land-scaped terraces, ponds, blooming trees and a three-storey pagoda. For something quite different, and especially for the younger set, visit the Yokohama Dreamland, built after the model of California's Disneyland and called by the Japanese a 'pleasure emporium'.

Kamakura
Yokohama is linked by fast and frequent trains to the capital in one direction and, in the other, to the historic city of Kamakura, only half an hour away. Kamakura was the political, administrative and religious centre of the country between 1192 and 1333, the so-

called Kamakura period. It was at this time that Yoritomo Minamoto (of the Genji clan) established his headquarters there, and where the first of many shogunates was founded by him. During the Kamakura period, which is remembered for its vigorous martial spirit, sculpture, epic literature and such manly crafts as metalwork flourished. It was then too that the first nationally based Buddhist sects came into being and their new temples were built in the region.

Today Kamakura is still adorned with no less than sixty-five Buddhist temples and other notable historic buildings. First and foremost, in the precincts of the Kotokuin temple belonging to the Jodo sect of Buddhism and about an eight-minute bus-ride from the main station, sits the imposing statue of the Kamakura Diabutsu (the Great Buddha). It is cast in bronze, weighs about ninety-three tonnes and is thirteen metres high; it is said to have been cast in 1252. This magnificent statue must be among the most frequently photographed and painted statues in the entire world, but in spite of such intense over-exposure to the popular gaze, the Buddha retains its essential spirit of calm and perfect detachment, the half-closed eyes signifying both everything and nothing.

Tucked away in the side-streets and the environs of Kamakura there are several other old temples and shrines that contain priceless treasures dating from the period of the city's supremacy. Among them is the Hase Kannon, famous for its eleven-headed statue of the Goddess of Mercy and the tallest wooden image in Japan. It is reputed to have been carved by a priest in the eighth century from the trunk of a camphor tree; the bell in the temple's precincts is especially beautiful and is classed as an Important Cultural Property.

The Gokurakuji temple, between Kamakura and the suburb of Katase houses no less than sixteen objects so designated. The temple was originally built in 1259 and several times damaged by fire, its treasures include stone and wooden statuary, bronze bells and well-wrought armour of the period. Kamakura also has a fine example of a Hachiman shrine, which was established in its present position in 1191. The enormous gingko tree to the left of its main steps marks the spot where the third Shogun was assassinated in 1219. In those far-off feudal days, it was the custom for soldiers to visit a Hachiman shrine, dedicated to the God of War, before they went into battle. For further temple-exploration, there are several others well worth a visit: the Engakuji, where there is a much-revered tooth reputedly belonging to the Gautema Buddha and Jochiji, a temple of the Rinzai sect which is picturesquely situated in a grove of cypresses.

But for all this, first-time visitors to Kamakura must be warned —the city is certainly not one that dwells on its past, and the ancient buildings it possesses are in secluded quiet corners that just keep at bay the bustle of the holidaymakers in the streets. For, on account of its proximity to Tokyo and Yokohama, it is one of the most popular seaside resorts in the country. Its crescent-shaped sandy beaches have facilities for most water sports and leisure activities, but don't expect to find much space to enjoy them—especially at summer weekends.

Just offshore from the main Katuse beach is an islet called Enoshima. It is connected to the mainland by a concrete bridge, and its quaint main street is crammed with souvenir shops that specialise in toys and ornaments made in local woods. It has a tropical garden, a small zoo and atop the islet's only hill, is a famous shrine of the Shinto faith, originally built in the twelfth century and containing a nude image of Benten, the Goddess of Beauty. Typically, you can reach the shrine in the traditional way by climbing pilgrim-fashion up three hundred worn, moss-covered steps—or you can ascend effortlessly on an escalator.

Mount Fuji

It is possible to visit the base of Mount Fuji on an organised day-excursion from either Tokyo or Yokohama. It's a fairly exhausting and rushed day, though better than not going at all. It's preferable, if you have the time, to spend a night or two in the area—which is now a National Park. For the record, the volcano is 3776 metres high and, although not one hundred and one per cent extinct, has only been known to erupt violently on fifteen occasions since the eighth century, the last being in 1707. Its familiar cone shape and almost perfect circular base is dear to the hearts of every loyal citizen. The Japanese call it 'peerless' and 'fabled', claiming that it never appears twice alike—a phantom, a cloud, a mystery as well as an ordinary volcanic cone.

It is not surprising therefore that Fuji has inspired many of the nation's artists and poets. Basho, the poet, gazed at it while standing by Lake Kawaguchi and wrote,

> On Kawaguchi's shore I muse
> While Fuji, through the changing mist,
> Presents all hundred views

When Fuji was officially worshipped as a sacred mountain, thousands of pilgrims clad in white tunics, straw hats and sandals climbed laboriously to its summit every summer as an act of faith. Upwards of 300,000 people still make the ascent annually, though only a few do so from strictly religious motives. The official climbing season is short — from 1 July to 31 August — and even at that time there is usually snow lingering on its summit. During this period, refreshments and accommodation (neither of very high quality) are available at the various stages of the ascent. There are six well-trodden routes to the top, which can take about nine hours to reach — it is rather more strenuous than an easy afternoon's stroll, so be warned! On clear days, the surrounding views — of countryside, peninsulas, isles and the distant Pacific — are quite stunning and perhaps worth all the effort. As the Japanese put it, 'It is as foolish not to climb Mount Fuji as to climb it twice in a life-time'.

Around the mountain's northern base lies the 'Five Lakes region', now considered part of a vast 'recreational complex' for Tokyo and therefore well supplied with facilities for camping, fishing, sailing and swimming. These mass-leisure developments are of recent origin and vary little from similar resort areas in many other countries — except that in Japan, ninety-nine percent of the heads in the water are black.

Hakone
Hakone is a long-established resort, lying to the south of Fuji and easily reached by special 'romance car trains' from either Tokyo or Yokohama. The whole district lies within the crater of an extinct volcano and in consequence numerous hot springs bubble irrepressibly from its various landscapes. At some of the best known gorges, such as Owakudani, 'The Valley of the Great Boiling' and Ojigoku, 'The Big Hell', and overpowering reek of sulphurous fumes floats forever upwards. A cable car that runs for four kilometres between the villages of Sounzan and Togendai on the shores of Lake Ashi offers a thirty-three minute, spectacular ride — with, at the end, a revolving observation platform for further panoramic views.

The place of major historical interest in the vicinity is the famous Hakone Shrine with its beautiful red gate (torii) standing close to the lakeside; many priceless relics are housed in the Treasure House beside the shrine building. The largest lake in the area called Ashi, along the shores of which the town of Hakone stands, is famous for its banks of spring-blooming azaleas and its Sakasa Fuji—that is, the inverted reflection of the famous mountain which is visible in the waters on clear, calm days. The Fujiya Hotel at Hakone is among the oldest-established and luxurious Western-style hostelries in the country and a great favourite with European tourists and residents. It has style, elegance, a lovely orchid house and it is, naturally, expensive.

Nikko

All the places so far described in this chapter are very well worth seeing. However, for those whose time for out-of-Tokyo tours is very limited, the top priority must be a visit to the shrines at Nikko, situated within a large National Park of lakes, rivers and wooded hills. The area is about 145 kilometres north of Tokyo and accessible from it in about two hours by rail. Numerous excursion buses also go there. Invariably, therefore, Nikko is fairly crowded, but the scenery and the shrines possess a large-scale grandeur that even a hundred busloads of enthusiastic tourists cannot spoil.

The Toshogu shrines in Nikko town is dedicated to Ieyasu, the founder of the Tokugawa shogunate. Approach to the shrines is across a sacred red bridge which was originally built in 1636; for over two hundred years after that only the Shogun and emissaries of the Emperor were allowed to cross it. Around the shrines are clusters of stately cryptomeria trees—the tall Japanese cedars that give extra grace and dignity to many of the country's ancient monuments. The architecture of the shrines is a mixture of Buddhist and Shinto, and the various gates, halls, pillars, offices and oratories that make up the whole impressive ensemble date from various historical periods. There is a five-storey pagoda, a sacred storehouse (with the celebrated simian trinity of 'Hear No Evil, Speak No Evil, See No Evil' carved on one panel), and the Kyozo, (the sutra library) where nearly seven thousand volumes of Buddhist sutras are kept in revolving bookcases.

To pick one spendid feature from many—look closely at the Yomeimon Gate, the Gate of Sunlight, replica from an older original and registered as a National Treasure in its own right. It is decorated with all manner of beasts, both real and fabled, with flowers, trees, birds and emblems and all outlined in such lavish and meticulous detail that it is also known as The Twilight Gate—for people tend to stand and gaze, lost in wonderment, for hours, until twilight falls. Indeed, each and every structure is so beautifully endowed with many-splendoured embellishments that it is best, on a first visit, to simply go and be dazzled, then return later with a comprehensive guide, for a more discriminating survey.

The Spring Festival of the Toshugu shrines, held on 17 and 18 May every year is one of the most exciting of the country's many. Its main attraction is the 'Thousand Person Procession' made up of groups of people carrying palanquins, weapons and musical instruments and dressed in costumes appropriate to the days of the shogunate. This is also a good time to enjoy the performance of sacred music and dances which, in the distant past, used to be held regularly in the shrine courtyards.

Magnificent as they are, the shrines are by no means all there is to see in the Nikko area. For, seventeen kilometres from Nikko, and up a scenic road that twists in forty-eight thrilling hairpin turns, is Chuzenji. The town, which stands 1270 metres above sea-level is on the shores of the clear, dark blue and beautiful Chuzenji Lake. From here, it is easy to visit the thundering waterfall, walk in the thickly wooded hills that surround its margins and visit the three neighbouring hot-spring resorts. The whole district is well served by buses, there are many pleasant hotels around—so a stay of two or three nights will allow you to explore the lovely scenery and really absorb the splendours of the shrines.

The Izu Peninsula
Last of the easily accessible sightseeing areas in this region is the Izu Peninsula. It lies south of the Hakone district and so has a slightly milder climate—people from Tokyo make excursions there to see the first plum blossoms of the year. The main route to the peninsula lies through Atami which, to most Westerners, represents ultra-modern Japan in its least attractive guise—a neon-lit glitter of amusement arcades, bars, skyscraper hotels and trashy souvenir shops, that has been rightly dubbed by Britons as the oriental equivalent of Margate!

Wise, really, to continue straight on to Ito, where there is a statue in commemoration of William Adams, that adventurous and resourceful pilot from Kent who helped to construct Japan's first ocean-going vessel. A place with better documented East-West connections is Shimoda, near the peninsula's tip. It was here that Townsend Harris, the first American diplomatic representative to Japan, came to live in 1856. His residence was a former temple called Gyokusenji which was restored by the American-Japanese

Society in the 1920s and now contains several interesting momentos of Harris's isolated sojourn as one of the only two Westerners in the country—the other being his young Dutch interpreter, Henry Heusken. The year after their arrival, Harris and Heusken made a ceremonial journey from Shimoda to Edo along part of the historic Tokaido highway to present their credentials to the Shogun. They were thus among the handful of foreigners who ever saw Japan in its sealed, totally feudal state before the West broke through its exclusiveness.

Harris travelled over unmade tracks in a most uncomfortable closed palanquin; nowadays, comfortable buses run the whole length of Izu, from Atami to the southern tip of Cape Iro, a rocky headland of stark cliffs with an observation tower and a lighthouse. It is possible to return by an inland route from the Cape to Shizenji, a popular hot-spring resort, and to go thence to Mito, the picturesque town on the peninsula's west coast—where there is a fascinating aquarium with dolphins and turtles. There are several other hot-spring spas in the vicinity, some of which are quite small and little developed commercially, though still within easy reach of Tokyo. They are not especially spectacular, but they do convey a feeling of that provincial, less sophisticated and modernised Japan that awaits the traveller who is able to strike out beyond the radius of the capital.

9 THE WAY TO THE SOUTH

The most spectacular scenic, though not the most direct way to the southern Japanese provinces is to first make a diversion south-west and visit part of the so-called 'Japanese Alps'. These are inland ranges of volcanic mountains that run from north to south through the wide central part of Honshu and are commonly known as The Roof of Japan. The region lies mostly within another national Park, a land of rushing rivers, dramatic peaks, conifered slopes and steep valleys. Concerted efforts have been made by the government to prevent the indiscriminate spread of unsightly developments, and the use of private cars is controlled. In some places, transportation is limited to buses and cable-cars and there are many well-marked trails for hikers. The happy result is that traffic congestion, air pollution and ugly new buildings are much less in evidence here than in some other resort areas.

The area is a mecca for those who love the out-of-doors—for alpine botanists, skiiers, climbers, walkers and hunters. In recent years, millions of urban-based Japanese have taken to these activities with huge enthusiasm, which helps to satisfy their yen for romantic derring-do. This spirit of bravado is particularly in evidence on the skiiing slopes where the young are likely to approach a mountain descent in the frame of mind of a kamikaze pilot—so if you are on skiis too, beware.

There are literally dozens of peaks that can be scaled or skiied upon, with varying degrees of difficulty, and the nearby winter-sports grounds are well equipped with chair lifts, rope ways and observation points—it is a national habit to seek out and officially designate the very best viewing points and then direct everyone to them in droves. On weekends and seasonal holidays the popular places are fairly crowded but, as is the case practically everywhere, you can find solitude if you get away from the well-beaten tracks. During off-peak times, it is possible to find quite cheap and adequate accommodation in ski lodges and hostels—but be prepared, naturally, to eat the local food.

For an overall bird's-eye view of the whole region, make for the Tateyama mountains, grandest of all the ranges, their heights sparkling with snow in winter and ablaze with alpine flowers in mid-summer. Tateyama mountain itself, like the country's other highest peaks, used to be an object of deep religious veneration and it is still known as one of the nation's three most sacred mountains.

On a direct rail and road route due south from Tateyama is Nagoya, on the Pacific bay of Ise and often called The Middle Capital. Long one of the country's three major industrial areas, the city was devastated during World War II because of its armaments factories, but it is now celebrated for the success of its post-war planning schemes and accommodates a population of more than two million. Nagoya orginally grew up around a number of feudal castles, the most famous dating from 1610 which the omni-present Shogun Ieyasu built for his son, Yoshinao, in the north-west of the city. The proud, five-storey structure, decorated with a famous pair of golden dolphins, was burned to the ground during the war, but was reconstructed in 1959 in accordance with the original specifications. The castle's main floors are now dedicated to the display of important cultural properties—the most interesting being a large series of paintings on sliding doors (fusamae) and on ceiling panels that were once in a mansion in the castle grounds. From the 'Lord's Room' on the top floor there is a good view of the surrounding plains reaching right to the distant Pacific.

Apart from the castle, the main attraction of the city, from the historically minded tourist's point of view, is the Tokugawa Art Museum that houses a major collection of art objects, records and heirlooms dating from the days of the shogunate. The best-known pieces are the 'Picture Scrolls of the Tale of the Genji' painted by a member of the Fujiwara family and registered as a National Treasure. Another nearby place of interest is the Gohyaku Rakan hall which contains five hundred unusually lively and varied images of Buddha's disciples.

If you happen to be in Nagoya in mid-April, incidentally, you will find yourself involved in a most exciting festival—that of the Toshogu shrine when gorgeous palanquins and floats are carried through the streets. If you are interested in the superb craftsmanship of the Japanese, Nagoya is a good place to visit factories where some of the country's finest porcelains and cloisonné ware is manufactured.

The most rewarding day-excursion from Nagoya is to Gifu, thirty kilometres north, an old castle town long celebrated for the ancient art of fishing with cormorants. The practice is carried on along the Nagara River at specified hours nearly every day between May and October. Nowadays it is rather more of a tourist attraction than an economically viable method of catching fish, nevertheless it makes for a very colourful and unusual spectacle. The fishermen go out in their boats and light flares slung from poles over the water to attract the fish; then the cormorants, with cords tied round their throats to prevent their swallowing, dive after them. The whole exercise is accomplished with great speed, efficiency and dexterity and the cormorants presumably never realise they are doing most of the work for nothing.

Continuing south along the coast from Nagoya, one reaches the grand Ise-Shima National Park located on the Ise Peninsula and possessed of a long, beautiful and varied coastline. The centre-piece of the park is the great Shrines of Ise that are located within the city of that name. They are the most sacred edifices in the country for the believers of Shintoism. The Inner Shrine (Naiku) is dedicated to the Sun Goddess, the creator of the nation, the founder of Japan's Imperial House; the Outer Shrine (Geku) is dedicated to the Goddess of Agriculture and Sericulture.

Considering the fundamental importance of these buildings and the reverence in which they are held by thousands of devout Shintoists, it is rather surprising for the Western visitor (more accustomed to the grandeur of Christian cathedrals) to see how simple and humble they appear. Both the shrines are built of plain cypress wood, raised on wooden columns and roofed with sloping thatch. They are highly significant however, not only from a religious standpoint, but because they represent the culmination of Japan's indigenous building style which prevailed in the fifth century before the introduction of Chinese architectural ideas. Every twenty years since the reign of the Emperor Tennu in the seventh century, it has been the custom to raze the buildings to the ground and build new ones on adjacent sites—a ceremony that last took place in 1973. This ingenious practice has ensured that the buildings are absolutely exact replicas of the ones demolished, and thus their traditional form has remained immaculately unchanged for twelve centuries.

At the Geku, which is surrounded by a magnificent grove of cedars, the sacred shrine dances called Kagura are regularly per-formed in an adjacent hall. The Inner Shrine is similar in its general arrangement, though even more sacred, and pilgrims customarily wash their hands and mouths in the waters of the Isuzu River as a gesture of purification before proceeding to it. Enshrined within it are the three sacred treasures—the Mirror, the Sword and the Jewel—that make up the regalia of the Imperial Throne. These simple and beautifully natural buildings, set in their peaceful, wooded surroundings, together with the myths and beliefs that accrue to them, epitomise in a very moving way the totally insular 'Japaneseness' of Japan as it once was in the very ancient days before the arrival of any foreign influences. For this reason alone, therefore, the Ise Shrines should rank high on every tourist's itinerary.

Immediately upon leaving the shrines one is rapidly returned to the modern world along the Iso-Shima Panoramic Skyline Toll Highway that runs along the edge of the Asama mountains to the port of Toba. Toba is now the starting point for tours through the National Park area and is therefore very tourist-oriented. It has lots of newly built hotels, and a seven-storey air-conditioned tourist centre where you can pick up useful guide pamphlets.

The town's chief attraction is the famous Pearl Island in the bay where Kokichi Mikimoto first managed to produce a cultured pearl. On the island, which is accessible by bridge or boat, there is a model pearl farm where the fascinating process of pearl culture is demonstrated, and the women (it has traditionally always been women) who dive for the oysters display their skills. At Toba itself they are principally a tourist 'sight', but, off the nearby Sugashima Islands about seven thousand women, wearing white cotton suits and face-masks, regularly earn their living by diving for the valuable marine products of the nearby shallow seas—which include abalone and lobsters as well as oysters.

From Toba comfortable excursion buses run to various lovely places along the Ise Peninsula, to the picturesque town of Wagu, home of many of the divers, and to Goza at the land's ultimate tip. From this rocky headland there are stunning views of blue Ago Bay which is usually crowded with rafts, below which the oysters are suspended.

10 KYOTO AND ENVIRONS

Kyoto is a southern city, climatically and temperamentally; its pace is slower and more relaxed than Tokyo, which is, of course, a mere nouveau rich upstart by comparison. For Kyoto was the capital of the country for more than ten centuries and is still its spiritual, historical and artistic centre, the place where many of Japan's leading scholars, craftsmen, artists and religious leaders chose to live.

According to the guide-pamphlets, the city '...teems with traditions and exudes an old-world atmosphere' and certainly it contains many of the most valuable artifacts and splendid buildings in the country. It is a cultural storehouse so rich that only by staying for at least a week could one hope to see everything that is important and inspiring. But if you cannot stay that long, concentrate on some of the more outstanding sights and still take time to potter round the back streets away from the packaged herds, for only in that way can you hope to get the true feel of a place that has played such a long and vital role in the country's history. (Incidentally, the Japan Tourist Board has realised the wisdom of this and has produced very helpful 'walking-guide maps' for visitors).

In the first centuries of Japan's habitation, the capital moved from place to place according to which one of the nomadic warring clans was in the temporary ascendant. The first permanent capital was fixed at Nara during the late seventh century; about a hundred years later a more permanent settlement was established from which present-day Kyoto has developed. As early as 805 this focus of human habitation was laid out in a formal grid plan facing south, in accordance with Chinese ideas of city planning. Nine main streets ran from east to west and were intersected by broad avenues, the central one leading to the palace, which was the seat of provincial and later national authority. Around the city perimeters was a deep ditch and an earth wall pierced by eighteen gates connecting to the main thoroughfares. This straighforward, sensible checkerboard design has influenced Kyoto's development ever since—one happy result of it is the comparative ease with which strangers can find their way about.

At first, the city was known as Heian-kyo, the 'capital of Eternal Tranquillity'; it was the home of a long succession of emperors who led secluded, pampered, ceremonial lives within the precincts of the imperial court. Few of these emperors wielded much real power and they were little more than puppets in the hands of various noble families who ruled as regents. Apart from power, these families were interested in a variety of cultural activities and the Heian period, between the ninth and twelfth centuries is still remembered as a time when arts and learning flourished in the capital.

Like most capitals however, Kyoto did not long remain a haven of tranquillity for the artistic and scholarly. Between the twelfth and sixteenth centuries it was freqently the scene of violent civil warfare as the rival clans fought for political supremacy. In 1569, Oda Nobunaga, the warrior-chieftain who began the task of restoring a centralised government to the entire country, entered the Imperial Capital and found it a scene of desolation—practically everything was destroyed. It was he and his immediate successor Hideyoshi (1563-98) who were responsible for the rebuilding of Kyoto to its state of earlier glory, using the same spacious planning concepts as in the earlier version. Most of the famous buildings and monuments there today date from that period; some are replicas of older originals.

When the Tokugawa Shoguns moved the seat of political authority to Edo in 1603, Kyoto naturally lost some of its importance and brilliance. But throughout the long period of the shogunate it remained the classical, religious and ceremonial capital and the centre of much cultural activity. Even today, emperors are enthroned in Kyoto and the Japanese speak of the place with great pride and devotion—unless you go there, they always tell foreigners, you haven't really seen Japan.

All this is true, but it is as well to know that today's Kyoto is not a sleepy of city full of nothing but cultural relics and a sense of the glorious past. It is the fifth largest city in the country, with a population exceeding a million and a half and about thirty million tourists visit it every year. This means, for one thing, that private tourist's cars in the city centre are liable for extra taxes and, for another, that accommodation is hard to find, especially in April, early autumn and at the time of the grand Gion city festival in mid-July. It is an important manufacturing centre too and so by no means immune to the problems of industrial pollution and congestion. The approach to it, through kilometres of recently built and typically ugly urban sprawl is not inspiring and, in the centre, the thunder of traffic is usually more insistent than the peal of temple bells.

But that is its worst aspect and there is a very great deal that is good. And confronted with so much, it is probably wise to start with three of the major attractions: Nijo Castle, the Sanjusangendo and Kinkakuji temples. They are included on practically all the numerous city tours—but to get the flavour of the place it is far preferable to go on foot when you can, for Kyoto is comparatively easy to negotiate and distances are not great.

Nijo Castle was originally built at the beginning of the seventeenth century by Ieyasu Tokugawa and was his residence whenever he visited Kyoto. It is one of the few really grand secular edifices in the country. Its grounds are surrounded by moats and turreted stone walls; at the entrance is an impressively massive iron-plated Eastern Gate leading to a spacious courtyard. Once inside however, the five inter-connected buildings that make up the whole are more like a gentleman's residence than a fortress. They consist of a large number of long, low reception rooms splendidly adorned with screen paintings, carved sliding doors and galleries, decorated ceilings, cross-beams with gold-plated nails. Many of the murals, mostly painted by members of the famous seventeenth-century Kano school depict fabled beasts and birds, flowers, trees and mysteriously misted landscapes and are quite exquisite. They are enhanced by the illumination of the subtle light that filters through the paper-screen windows.

Kyoto has always been a focal point for Japanese Buddhism, and a variety of Buddhist sects—whose leaders, in earlier days, were often at loggerheads over doctrinal and political issues— have made their headquarters there. From the Heian period onwards their monasteries and temples have been among the finest examples of Japan's religious architecture; they have also been repositories for the most prized works of painting and literature, centres of philosophical learning and training grounds for young monks, artists and calligraphers.

Today, there are about 1500 temples in the city, thirty of them headquarters of Buddhist sects. Probably the best known and certainly the most frequently illustrated and photographed of them all is the Sanjusangendo. The temple's main hall contains the beautifully carved wooden image of the Thousand-Handed Kannon (Goddess) in a sitting posture and accompanied by statues of Twenty-Eight Faithful Followers (all designated as National Treasures). Flanking the main statue, are no less than a thousand smaller images of the same goddess. All these were painstakingly carved during the thirteenth century by the famous sculptor Unkei and his son Tankei—who inspired several other religious artists of the period. The concept of so very many identical images sounds rather excessive and is a little overwhelming at first sight. But the view of row upon row of these silent, gilded figures is extremely impressive.

The Kinkakuji, the Temple of the Gold Pavilion, in the north-east of the city, is probably the most internationally known of all Kyoto's famous buildings. Partly, this is because its original was burned down in 1950 by one of the young priests who lived there. This event later formed the theme of a powerful novel by Yukio Mishima who showed that in his life the priest was fascinated by ideas of destruction and self-destruction as he himself had always been. The original building, its walls covered with gold foil, was built as a villa in 1397 by the third Shogun, Yoshimitsu Ashikaya, (1358-1408) who retired there, and it was designed and placed so as to make a harmonious whole with the landscaped garden surrounding it.

After the Shogun's death, the villa, in accordance with his will, became a Buddhist temple and for the next 550 years it remained a centre of meditation and prayer for Buddhist priests, its upper storey being used as an oratory. The present building, an exact replica of this original, was built in 1955 and looks just as beautiful, especially in bright sunshine, when its golden reflection, topped by a bronze phoenix, glints in the waters of the small lake in front of it.

A sort of companion-piece to the Kinkakuji is the Ginkakuji or Silver Pavilion which was built fifty years later. It too was originally built as a country villa for a Shogun and converted to a temple. It is not actually covered with a silver patina as was the original intention, but it is certainly beautiful, with bell-shaped windows in the upper storey and upturned eaves that produce a harmonious combination of Chinese and Japanese architectural styles. There is a lily pond in the garden and a tiny room that is said to be one of the oldest in the country.

The most influential Buddhist sect that took root in Kyoto was Zen (see chapter 2) and there are several Zen temples in Kyoto;

most welcoming to the tourist is the Daitoku-ji, the sect's head-quarters, a temple complex set in eleven hectares of ground. There are a number of ceremonial halls, carved gates, tea-houses and small temples containing precious works of art.

During the medieval period, the masters of Zen formulated exercises in contemplation and spirituality from which developed practices such as Noh dancing, flower arranging and the tea ceremony that have been part of Japan's cultural heritage ever since. Teachers of Zen also formulated original ideas for the land-scaping of their temple gardens and several of these still exist in Kyoto. There is one at Daitoku-ji, but the best known are at the Nanzenji and the Ryoanji temples. Created to conform to the Zen principles of stark simplicity and purity, they contain only rocks and raked sand, and are in every way a far cry from the flower-packed patches we think of as gardens. As the Japan Tourist Board warns therefore, foreign visitors may fail to appreciate the full spiritual significance of such refined arrangements and see no more than flat space strewn with sand and stones—but it is certainly worth while going to find out.

The Jodo Shin was one of the Buddhist sects that originated in Kyoto, its headquarters are still there and its Nishi Honganji temple contains some of the city's finest artistic treasures. The Hondo (meaning 'main hall') reconstructed in 1760 is splendidly decorated by masters of the Kano school who successfully blended Japanese and Chinese painting styles and some of whose members were appointed official painters to the Tokugawa shogunate. The Daisho (Founders) Hall contains images of the sect's founder and subsequent abbots that are most compelling. Permission to view the rest of the treasures—many of which are most rare and beautiful—can be obtained on personal request from the temple's office. Included among the collection is one of the most perfect and oldest remaining Noh stages in the country which is now designated a National Treasure.

Many of the other Buddhist temples in the city contain wall-paintings of great vigour and nobility that date from the tenth to twelfth century; among them are Shoren-in (look particularly for the fierce God of fire), the Daigo-ji (where there is a wonderfully mysterious image of the Goddess of Mercy), and the Kyogoku-ji —with a most colourful representation of the Buddha surrounded by flower offerings. The hall of this last edifice, incidentally, has a most attractively ornamented roof, dominated by the grinning head of a monster intended to ward off evil spirits.

One of the most appealing and famous of all the Buddhist temples in the area is the Byodoin which is situated in Uji City, an easy thirty-minute train trip from Kyoto and also included in several of the Kyoto-based tours. The main hall of the Byodoin was built in 1053 and is about the finest remaining example of the religious architecture of that period. It is called the Amida-do, the Phoenix Hall, because its design represents that mythological bird and atop its central roof soar male and female phoenixes cast in bronze. The inside is elaborately decorated in gold and red with Buddhist paintings by the court painter Takuma on doors and panelling. The Byodoin also contains two National Treasures: a gracious statue of the Amida Buddha attributed to the famous sculptor Jocho and considered to be his masterpiece, and a beautifully wrought bronze bell with relief designs of maidens and lions that suggest a Korean influence.

On an islet in the River Uji just to the east of the temple grounds stands a thirteen-storey stone pagoda that was originally erected in the thirteenth century by a Buddhist priest; it was re-built using the original remains a full seven centuries later. If you happen to be in the vicinity on a summer evening between June and August you can probably watch a demonstration of traditional cormorant fishing in the Uji River.

It must be acknowledged that many casual visitors to Kyoto tend to run out of enthusiasm for temple-exploration before they run out of temples—for there are literally hundreds of them and nearly all have some interesting architectural features and contain artifacts and paintings of great beauty and historical value. Directions on how to reach them are well set out in the city's maps and pamphlet-guides produced by the Japan Tourist Office and there are also several books in English available which describe each one very comprehensively.

But Kyoto has many other, secular, attractions to offer the visitor, for it was a royal as well as a religious capital for centuries. The most impressive evidence of this is to be seen at the Imperial Palace, the Kyoto Gosho which is enclosed in eleven hectares of parkland. It became the official imperial residence in 1331 since which time twenty-eight successive emperors lived there—and many of the buildings were destroyed by fire and rebuilt. The new building, modelled on earlier versions, was erected in the nineteenth century.

Visitors can go to the palace accompanied by a palace guard and there is usually an English-speaking interpreter in attendance. The gateways of the Gosho are magnificent even by Japanese

standards; the main south gate, called the Kenrei-mon is made of
zelkova wood with a roof of cypress bark and only the reigning
Emperor is allowed to pass through its doors. The main edifice,
the Shishinden or Ceremonial Hall was used for imperial
enthronements and contains the Emperor's throne. It is a threefold
dais draped with rich silk curtains and topped with an octagonal
roof adorned with a Chinese-style phoenix. To the north-west of
the shishinden is the Seiryoden, the 'Serene and Cool Chamber'
so called because of the stream running under its steps. Built of
Japanese cypress and embellished everywhere with the imperial
crest, the sixteen-petalled chrysanthemum, this lovely building
also contains some excellent screen paintings of the Tosa school.
The tour of inspection (which is rather limited) ends with a walk
along the Giyoden corridor to the Pond Garden with a fairly large
expanse of water surrounding picturesque pine-clad islets and with
a stone-paved shore.

Kyoto's other most attractive secular building is the Katsura
Villa which is considered the absolutely supreme example of the
Shoin style of domestic architecture and landscape gardening. It
is simple, harmonious and perfect, built with basic, unadorned
materials—wood, tile, paper—and it simply exudes *wabi*, i.e. quiet
taste. One needs to apply in advance to the Japan Tourist Board
for permission to visit Katsura and visiting hours are restricted,
but it is worth the effort. The villa is situated away from the city
centre in quiet and lovely surroundings beside the Katsura River
and it was created for an imperial prince during the seventeenth
century. Its grounds are really its most appealing feature and were
designed especially to stroll about and relax in while contemplating
the beauties of the changing seasons. There are several small wooden
buildings serendipitiously placed in relation to grassy knolls and
groves, one for each season of the year. One of them is a particularly
famous tea-house, so well designed in relation to the light that,
the Japanese claim, there is never a dark corner in it.

The villa itself, made of the most simple natural materials, is
divided into three sections and several rooms, one of which contains
a lovely painting by the seventeenth-century master Naonobu Kano
with the delightful title of 'Seven Recluses in a Bamboo Grove'. It
is hard to imagine that anyone ever lived very comfortably in
Katsura; it is too austere and perfect, an abstraction that could
scarcely allow for the normal clutter of a home. But is very revealing
of that part of the Japanese temperament which is devoted to the
qualities of restraint, economy and the refinement of the natural

in matters aesthetic.

Kyoto is the principal centre for the traditional arts of the nation and many of the skills in which the Japanese so excel, such as embroidery, lacquerware, the weaving of silk, carving of ivory, making of fans, decoration of porcelain, all of which have been practised by the city's craftsmen for centuries. To get some idea of this aspect of Kyoto's life, visit the recently opened Municipal Centre of Trade and Industry at Okazaki Park. There you can see not only the most exquisite examples of all kinds of handicrafts — in bamboo, silk, paper, ceramics etc. — but also fascinating demonstrations of the old-established methods of manufacture.

Of similar interest is the Nishiju Textile Museum which contains splendid arrays of textiles both ancient and modern and records the story of the Nishiju silk-weaving industry from its beginnings. Along the alleys nearby you can hear the click of weaving looms that come from the domestic workshops still concentrated in that area, where beautiful shawls, scarves, dress materials and draperies are made. You may well be tempted to purchase some of these, or other specialist goods such as the lustrous dyed fabrics patterned with complicated designs that date back over a thousand years. Other good buys are porcelains (collectively known as kyo-yaki) and lacquerware, especially the gold and silver work called maki-e in which gold and silver dust is mixed with the lacquer base.

If, after so many crafts, you feel like an instant run-down on the traditional arts, visit Gion Corner, set up by the Foreign Visitor's Club in the Gion entertainment quarter. Here you can see regular demonstrations of flower-arranging, tea ceremony, bunraku puppet plays, ancient court dances and kyogen — the classical comic interludes that lighten the performance of Noh plays.

One of the three greatest festivals in Japan takes place in the Gion district between 16 and 24 July. It dates right back to the ninth century and consists of huge decorated floats parading along the streets accompanied by musicians playing traditional instruments such as gongs and flutes. On account of its long and eventful history, Kyoto's calendar is in fact crammed with festivals and 'special events' and you can hardly fail to encounter one, for there is something nearly every day — details of which are listed in the monthly guides issued by the Japan Tourist Board. Among the most interesting are the archery contests held in the outer corridor of Sanjusangendo Hall which is a competition that dates back to the sixteenth century; the medieval pantomime-farces with musical accompaniments that are staged at the Mibu temple at the end of April; the Hollyhock

Festival in mid-May during which the traditional imperial processions to the city's shrines are re-enacted; the Jidai Matsuri or Festival of Eras held at the Heian Shrine on 22 October to commemorate the founding of Kyoto in 794.

Prior to that date, the nation's capital for about seventy years was Nara. Forty-one kilometres to the south, it can be easily reached by train in an hour or on one of the day-long bus-tours that feature 'instant-Nara' side-trips from Kyoto. During its heyday in the eighth century, Nara was grander than it has been since; it was a flourishing centre of Buddhism, with many of the temples owning large estates in their own right and having considerable political power. Much has been destroyed or fallen into disrepair since then and now there are a number of unfortunate modern hotel developments, parking lots and even a 'Fantasy Land' disfiguring the scene. Nevertheless, many traces of Nara's former glories remain and it is worth more time than is usually allowed on the one-day trips.

Several of the city's most splendid sights are conveniently grouped around the Nara central park, which, incidentally also contains a large herd of tame and much-photographed deer. The first outstanding edifice is the five-storey pagoda of the Kofukuji temple that was rebuilt in 1426 in faithful imitation of the original that dated from the eighth century. It is about fifty metres high, the second tallest pagoda in the country and now designated as a National Treasure.

The buildings within the temple's precincts are the headquarters of the Hosso sect of Buddhism and include an impressive central hall, the Chu Kondo containing a wooden image of the historical Buddha and his followers and the To-Kondo which was rebuilt early in the fifteenth century and has a statue of Buddha as healer flanked by two most beautiful lacquer-wood figures representing sunlight and moonlight. Near the Chu-Kondo is the modern building of the Kokuho-kan, the Hall of National Treasures that houses several groups of Buddhist-inspired statuary from the Heian period and two statues attributed to Jokei, a sculptor of the Kamakura period.

Kojukuji is one of the so-called 'Sever Great Temples of Nara', and you may not have the time or inclination to visit them all; but be sure to visit at least two others. First, the Todaiji temple, headquarters of the Kegon sect, and famous for its possession of the world's largest bronze statue of the Daibutsu (Buddha) which is housed in the world's largest wooden structure—at least, that is what the Japanese claim. There is no need to describe the exact dimensions here, for they appear in every tourist hand-out; the Japanese never miss a chance to list such points. But in any case, measurements themselves do not convey the tremendous visual impact which the Daibutsu makes as one enters the Hall—an utterly enormous, towering, yet benevolent-seeming figure seated cross-legged on a huge bronze pedestal made of fifty-six separate lotus petals.

After the largest, go to the oldest temple extant in the country. It is called the Horyuji and dates from the seventh century. It is about nine kilometres outside the main city and easily accessible by train, bus or taxi. The temple, headquarters of the Shotuku sect, comprises forty-five buildings, their periods of construction dating from the seventh to the sixteenth century. Of these, seventeen are known as National Treasures, the rest as Cultural Properties. Among the many features of interest look first for the fierce guardian gods in the niches of the Chumon Gate that dates from the time of the temple's first construction. Similar examples of such statues can be seen elsewhere, but these are both the oldest known and the most powerfully carved of them all.

The Kondo, main hall, houses several Buddhist images in wood and bronze and some stunning frescoes designed by unknown artists. Many other pieces of wooden and bronze statuary and relics such as masks used for religious dances can be seen in the modern Treasure Hall which also has displays of scroll paintings, brocades and bronze miniatures. The most commonly admired images there are two Kannons, one exquisitely carved in sandalwood, the other believed to have had the power of changing bad dreams into good.

As a change from so many overwhelming Buddhist presences, there is the Shosoin Treasure Repository which looks rather like a log-cabin on stilts but which contains more than nine thousand articles of great beauty and craftsmanship, including jewels, musical instruments, writing materials, costumes, masks, weapons and everyday utensils dating from the brief period of Nara's supremacy. There is also one very beautiful vermilion-lacquered Shinto shrine in the city called the Kasuga. It was originally founded in 768 and was the tutelary shrine of the powerful Fujiwara family. The Kasuga is actually four smallish shrines surrounded by trees and the approach to them is through two magnificent high red torii and along an avenue lined with some three thousand bronze and stone lanterns. These lanterns are all lighted twice a year—once in early February and again in August

—when they present a really exciting spectacle.

After so much sightseeing, you might remember that Nara has one of the pleasantest old-style hotels in the country. Called the Nara, its rooms overlook a small lake and are high-ceilinged and rather dignified—a pleasant change from the usual preponderance of international plush-and-chrome. There is a good, but usually crowded dining and grill room.

One of the country's lesser known excellent museums and one of its 'Outstanding Scenic Places' are within easy reach of Nara. The former, eight kilometres south of the city, is in the head-quarters of the Tenrikyo Shinto sect (see chapter 2) and contains fascinating pieces of classical art from China, Korea and the Middle East and an equally good collection of folk art from many Eastern and even African countries. The scenic place is the Tsukigase Plum Groves where plum trees blossom in grand abundance throughout March and early April; the sight is a collectors' item for the nations' thousands of flower-lovers and has been celebrated many times in verse and song.

There are two other interesting out-of-city excursions to be made in the region, one to the Hozu Rapids that flow from Kameoka to Arashiyama, about sixteen kilometres from Kyoto. Flat-bottomed boats manned by three oarsmen negotiate the rapids, winding skilfully (and safely) down-river between huge rocks and verdant hills. Near the end of the trip, a great whirlpool adds a splash of extra excitement to the thrills of the journey.

The other rewarding trip that can be made from either Kyoto or Nara is to Lake Biwa and the town of Otsu. The lake, the largest in the country, is shaped like the musical instrument of the same name, and it has been featured in many famous Japanese paintings and woodblock prints. The surroundings of the lake, designated as a Quasi-National Park, are pleasantly wooded hills dotted with old temples, bridges and gardens. It is possible to travel by train or bus along the lake-shores on either side, stopping at some of the most important sights en route. The town of Otsu is rich in early historical associations for it was the seat of the Imperial Court for brief periods during the second and seventh centuries. Excursion boats run from Otsu to the eight finest selected views of Lake Biwa that include rapids, mountains, an island and a castle.

The town of Otsu itself has now become an industrial centre, and the same fate, in a more dramatic form, has also overtaken Osaka. It too is a place of great historical and cultural interest, but it is fast becoming the concrete heart of a megalopolis which sprawls towards and threatens to soon include Kyoto, Nara and Kobe. Large-scale industrial complexes for the manufacture of chemicals, textiles, iron and steel products and food-processing are centred in Osaka which also has a huge dock area that handles about forty percent of Japan's total exports. The city is over-crowded and most of its horizons are unlovely; it is proud of such recent acquisitions as vast underground shopping complexes, sports stadiums, trade-show halls and flashy amusement quarters. In short, it is not the place to linger long if your main enthusiasm is for oriental antiquities, picturesque buildings, fresh air or serenity.

But the city has a grand history and the most obvious evidence of this is its castle in the north-east section. The original structure was built between 1582 and 1585 by the warrior-leader Hideyoshi Toyotomi who realised Osaka's strategic importance. In its day, it was the greatest of all the nation's castles and surrounded with immense ramparts and deep moats. Hideyoshi, who was also a patron of the arts, amassed a fine collection of treasures there— bowls and stands of gold lacquer, painted screens, carvings of wood and ivory, and some of these are on display inside.

In 1615 the grand edifice was burned to the ground by Ieyasu Tokugawa who seized the shogunate from Hideyoshi's son, Hideyori. The latter committed suicide with his mother as the castle was burning—a scene which is often dramatically re-enacted on the Kabuki stage. Later, the castle was re-built and remained intact until 1868 when it was again set on fire by the Tokugawa troops before they fled the city at the time of the restoration of the Emperor Meiji. The present structure, made of ferro-concrete, is, like many other historical buildings, a faithful and loving re-creation of the original. It towers fifty-seven metres high and, from the top, offers extensive views of the heavily built-up and usually smoke-laden districts below. Inside the castle there are various exhibits of historical interest and the land surrounding it is one of the city's few green and open spaces. At night, the castle is most effectively illuminated.

The other main attraction that Osaka offers the average tourist, who has only a limited interest in modern industrial develop-ments, is performances of Bunraku puppet theatre. This form of theatrical entertainment was extremely popular in Osaka in the late seventeenth and eighteenth centuries when the city was a lively cultural centre, much fequented by writers, artists and dramatists—the most famous playwright Monzaemon Chikamatsu was born there. Nowadays, the only two theatres that regularly show Bunraku plays are the National Theatre in Tokyo and the Asahiza theatre in Osaka where it is performed by a dedicated troupe of men, many of them from families with generations of experience in the puppeteering art.

11 THE INLAND SEA REGION

The Inland Sea is a complicated combination of land and water which is unique in the world. It is actually a chain of five seas linked by channels (its Japanese name is 'Sea within Channels'), the surfaces of which are dotted with about three thousand small islands and islets. Its mild, shallow waters team with marine life of all kinds, citrus fruits grow in abundance along its shores and the various indented coastlines offer many lovely aspects of white sands, blue waters, gnarled pines and granite rocks.

On many of the smaller islands and along the shores you can see people whose appearance—in smocks and wide straw hats—makes a pleasant change from all those nattily-dressed office workers in the cities. They are engaged in a variety of outdoor activities: fishing (in particular for the sea bream and mackerel which are much-prized local delicacies); collecting salt; cultivating oranges, persimmons, peaches, soy beans, olives; quarrying for granite. Some of the smallest islands are uninhabited, but their terraced fields are cultivated by farmers who come to them by boat.

The most agreeable time to visit the area is in early summer or early autumn when the flowers, the trees and the climate are at their best. Needless to say, most of the Inland Sea is now designated as a National Park, and there are, in consequence, ever-expanding facilities for sightseeing and water-sports, plus a growing number of hotels that cater to foreign visitors (though many fewer than in central Honshu).

The most satisfactory way to appreciate the visual delights of these supreme water-scapes is obviously to travel over the water itself. And the Japanese have taken full account of this by operating a number of regular services in luxury cruise ships, steamers, ferry-boats and hydrofoils between all the main ports. Package cruises of up to five days duration cover the entire area between Osaka and Beppu on Kyushu, and there are many choices of sightseeing trips of varying duration—between one and a half to fourteen hours. In addition, small boats run ad hoc services between some of the smaller islands. So, as distances are fairly small, you can see most of the region's main attractions comfortably within a fairly short time.

Shikoku, which is the smallest of Japan's main islands, lies on the southern shores of the Inland Sea and is readily accessible from Honshu both by sea and by air—it has four airports. By Honshu standards, Shikoku is relatively undeveloped; it is watered by several large rivers and it has long been an object of pilgrimage for Japanese Buddhists. There are no less than eighty-eight Buddhist temples on the island and it used to be traditional for thousands of white-robed pilgrims to trudge round them all during the spring. Now there are few pilgrims in evidence and most people go from one temple to another in special coaches. Takamatsu, an old castle town, is the best starting-off point for sightseeing excursions of this sort.

The largest city on Shikoku is Matsuyama, easily accessible from Takamatsu. With a population of about 350,000, it's a pleasing educational and cultural centre and with several temples and monuments of historical interest, including a castle that is one of the best preserved in the country. One of its oldest spa-resorts, Dogo, is situated in the nearby hills. If you don't get to Nagoya, you can see similar demonstrations of fishing with cormorants at Iyo-Ozu, a town to the south-west of Matsuyama where it is carried on throughout the summer months.

Two of the many other islands in the Inland Sea region that are well worth visiting are Awaji and Shodo. They are situated off the eastern shores and are accessible by high-speed boats from the mainland, and they are favourite ports-of-call for excursion ships. Awaji has a population of some 50,000 but it is not very built up, except at Sumoto which is its largest city. (The nature of Sumoto, in comparison with cities like Osaka, may be guessed from the fact that its chief products are officially listed as: buttons, roofing tiles, dried sardines and onions.) A forty-minute bus journey will take you to the island's best known tourist 'sight'—the roaring whirlpools that are best viewed from Cape Naruto. From Mount Senzan, a few miles north-west of Sumoto there are spectacular views of all the surrounding highlands and islands.

Shodo island, which is considerably smaller than Awaji, also boasts one particularly spectacular natural phenomenon—the Kankakei, literally the Cold and Misty Gorge, which is a group of strangely eroded rocks and peaks. The gorge is a mass of azaleas and of brilliant red maples in the appropriate seasons. The area that lies between Shodo and Tomonoura on the mainland is considered the most beautiful section of the whole region by the discriminating Japanese. In general, the chief delights here are scenic rather than cultural and artistic, though there are some historical buildings of note and some fine paintings and sculptures in the museums. Similarly, it is not the place to buy the country's most exquisite art and craft products, but there are some tempting regional artifacts to consider, specially those made from coral, shell and paper. Dried and preserved fruits are a speciality as are the dried fish, particularly bonito and tunny—though these are very much an acquired taste for most Westerners.

A main port of embarkation for the Inland Sea is Kobe on the Bay of Osaka. Like Yokohama, Kobe has a long history of association with foreigners and was one of the first treaty ports opened to foreign trade over a hundred years ago. In those days, the arrival of a trading steamer from Shanghai was a considerable event, but today more than 10,000 ocean-going vessels per year pass through the port, which has become a hive of commercial activity and a centre for the iron and steel industry and ship-building.

People from many nations have taken root in Kobe over the years and among them has been a fair sprinkling of Chinese and Koreans. In consequence the Korean and Chinese fare available there is rated about the best in the country and there are also reasonable Italian, French and American restaurants, and even an 'old English tavern' with real wooden beams for the home-sick Britisher. Kobe is also famed for the quality of its beef (which is generally not very high in Japan) and its local brews of beer and saké are prized by connoisseurs.

Compared to some Japanese cities, Kobe does not offer a great deal in the way of historical and cultural interest, but it has two good museums: the Namban Art Museum has some very jolly early Western-style paintings by Japanese artists, including some depicting Westerners; the Hakutsuru Art Museum has a famous collection of old ceramics and Chinese bronzes. There are lots of pleasant places to walk in Kobe—over the hills and in the parks— and enjoyable excursions to be made to nearby hill resorts and spas. For something quite different, go to Takarazuka and see the nationally renowned all-women opera group at the town's Grand Theatre.

From Kobe, a good train service runs westward, near the shores of the Inland Sea towards Kyushu. The most interesting stop-offs are at Himeji, where there is a White Heron castle originally built of wood, and (bypassing industrialised Okayama), Kurashiki which was once the centre of the region's rice trade. It is an old city renowned for its excellent Folkcraft and Archeological Museums which are re-modelled rice granaries standing on the shores of a tree-lined river. The displays of locally produced pottery, rugs, mats, woodcarvings and textiles in the former are most appealing and show the different style of ingenious craftsmanship that has developed in the western and southern provinces.

The next major station along the same line has a name with very sombre international connotations: Hiroshima. On 6 August 1945 at 8.15 in the morning the city was flattened and blown apart by the world's first atomic bomb raid, and more than 200,000 people were killed. Two years later, the first Peace Festival on the theme of 'No More Hiroshima' was held and every year since then a commemorative gathering has taken place in the city's Peace Park. There is a Memorial Museum in the park that contains exhibits and descriptions of the catastrophe by eye-witnesses and sufferers and this should certainly be visited. During the past twenty-five years, Hiroshima has been completely re-built in modern style and its population is now more than twice what it was before the bomb fell. As befits the new, onward-looking Japan, it contains the usual complement of shopping centres, skyscraper blocks, entertainment quarters and super highways.

A thirty-minute journey by bus and ferry out of Hiroshima will take you to Miyajima, probably the most-photographed of all the photogenic islands of the Inland Sea. It is small and mountainous and its special claim to fame is the ancient Itsukushima Shrine, which was once the spiritual centre of worship for the doughty Taira clan. It is built on supports extending into the water, and, at high tide, the reflection of the vermilion woodwork is mirrored most beautifully in the surface below. This shrine, with the large red camphor wood torii that rises from the sea nearby, has been an object of pilgrimage for centuries and is acclaimed as one of Japan's 'Three Most Beautiful Sights'. It is beautiful at any time of the year, but never more so than in the early spring when the island's cherry trees are in dazzling bloom, or when, on festival occasions, all the stone lanterns within its precincts are lit.

Most of the tourist interest in this part of Japan has, naturally and rightly, focussed on the Inland Sea and its surrounding mainland. However, if you have the time and want to see a part of the country which is scenically lovely and has been less affected than most by the growth of national industry and international trade and the incursions of 'western barbarians' head north by rail from Hiroshima, across the undeveloped central mountainous region to the city of Matsue.

One of the very few Westerners to actually live in Matsue during the nineteenth century was the Irish-American writer Lafcadio Hearn, who taught at the local college. The house in which he lived in 1890 has remained much as it was, and there is a Memorial Hall next door commemorating his life and work. Hearn's romances and ghost stories have not all withstood the test of time very well, but some of his essays provide fascinating insights into the Japanese character as he saw it, and are a valuable commentary on this earlier and more tentative period of East-West encounters. There is also an impressive old castle at Matsue which was first constructed in the seventeenth century, and not far away, an attractive and unspoilt scenic area around the wooded Lake Shinji.

It is no great distance from either Matsue or Hiroshima to Shimonoseki, the westernmost town of Honshu, which, because of its stategic location, has been the scene of several historic battles. The most famous, in Japanese annals, took place along the town's shoreline in 1185, when most of the Taira (also called Heike) clan was exterminated by the Minamoto (Genji) clan—a bloody encounter that has been the theme of several spirited paintings. In Western annals, Shimonoseki is more often associated with the date of 1865 when members of the Choshu clan who wanted 'to expel the barbarian invaders from the country' began to fire on Western ships that were passing through the Shinomoseki Straits. In huge retaliation, a combined fleet of British, American, French and Dutch warships bombarded the little town for three days and caused great damage. Today Shimonoseki is peaceful and not very memorable; perhaps the main reason for going there is because of its proximity to Kyushu just across the water, where a different aspect of the Japanese scene begins.

12 THE FAR SOUTH

Kyushu, Japan's southernmost island, is a little milder, lusher, softer than the rest of the country. In common with the southern regions of most countries, the pace is rather quieter, the atmosphere more languid, the colours brighter, the people somewhat more volatile—though the oft-used term, 'the Latins of Japan' is something of an exaggeration. For the traveller, it is an island with a great deal to offer: places of historical interest, cultural treasures of its own special kind, beautiful coastlines, foaming hot-springs and dramatic mountain scenery much of it contained within one of its six National Parks. Kyushu is connected to south-west Honshu by two rail tunnels and a suspension bridge; it also has six airports which link its main population centres to the rest of the country.

Because of its proximity to China and Korea, Kyushu became the centre of international trade and cultural communication from the fourth century onwards. In the thirteenth century, Kublai Khan twice tried to conquer the land and fierce battles between the Japanese and the Mongol invaders were fought in north Kyushu, the latter being driven back eventually. In their last attempt made in 1281, incidentally, the Mongol fleet was utterly destroyed by a devastating typhoon, there after known as 'kamikaze', the 'Divine Wind'.

When the redoubtable Jesuit missionary, Francis Xavier reached the country in 1549 he concentrated his missionary efforts to Kyushu. He did not succeed in converting the island to his branch of Christianity, but it still remains the national centre of Catholicism. During the closed period of the shogunate, Kyushu's most beautiful port, Nagasaki was the only 'Japanese window' left slightly open to the rest of the world, and the port has remained an important international trading and cruising centre ever since.

Fukuoka, another old trading port, is now the largest and most prosperous city on Kyushu, the centre of the northern manufacturing and mining belt and the busiest gateway to the island by air. Because of this it is by no means the most attractive place on

Kyushu, but it makes a good starting point for seeing the rest of the island and is one of three jumping-off places for the Okinawa islands (the others are Tokyo and Osaka).

If you are there for a while, have a look at the varied selections of artistically designed Hakata dolls that are made of fine clay and delicately painted to represent court ladies, warriors and gods. Also famous are the Hakata silk textiles that are most subtly coloured and have been specialities of the local craftsmen for centuries. The city is also a good place to buy Satsuma-yaki, the unusual, crackled-surface porcelain ware which was first made in Kyushu in the seventeenth century. This ware is generally regarded by collectors as the very finest of all the lovely ceramics the country produces.

If you are particularly interested in the early eastern encounters with 'western barbarians' make a short side-trip from Fukuoka to the hilly little island of Hirado that lies within the boundaries of the Saikai National Park. Hirado was the first port opened by the Japanese to foreign traders in 1550 and Dutch, English and Spanish merchants built factories there. Unfortunately, there is little evidence of this left, but the Hirado castle has been well restored.

A longer and very interesting side-trip from Fukuoka is to the islands of Okinawa and regular air services (flight time one and a half hours) link the two places. The capital of Okinawa is Naha, with a population of some 306,000 and it is the economic and cultural centre of the four-island group—Okinawa itself, Miyako, Yaeyama and Daito. These islands have had a checkered history since the fourteenth century when they lost their independence to the Chinese. For the next 250 years, the island kingdom was peaceful, though politically and culturally dominated by the vast 'Middle Kingdom' across the sea. But in 1609 it was over-run by Japanese warrior-bands from Kyushu and from then on owed allegiance to both China and Japan, though its official language remained Chinese. Japan took over complete rule of the country in 1872 and lost it to the American armed forces during World War II—some of the bitterest fighting of the Pacific battle-area took place there in 1945. By the terms of a new peace treaty between Japan and the United States signed in 1972, the islands reverted to Japanese control, and are now administered as a Japanese prefecture.

The rural districts of all the Okinawan islands are quite beautiful: green hills covered with lush vegetation, plantations of cocunut palms, sweet potatoes, pineapples, warm coral-reef seas and white-sand beaches. And for this very reason of course, resorts are already being developed by the space-hungry Japanese. The main cities of Naha and Okinawa are brash and unattractive with many reminders of the time of the long American occupation, though they are becoming rapidly 'Japanised'. The main avenue of Naha has rows of department stores, bars, boutiques and restaurants and has become a mini-Ginza.

There are no train services on any of the islands, but regular bus services and taxis (often on a shared-tour basis) take people to the main sights. One of the most popular excursions is to Moon Beach, where glass-bottomed boats are for hire that enable you to view the brilliant colours of the underwater tropical world of the bay, and there is also a Marine Observatory in the park. Another trip is to the Nakagusuku Park where there are the remains of a fifteenth-century castle and, nearby, the Nakamura House which is an attractive and unique example of a typical Okinawan house built over two hundred years ago.

South from Naha is the Old Battlefield Quasi-National Park which has sixty-seven monuments to the war dead and there is also the famous Hill 89 on which many members of the Japanese High Command committed mass suicide in proper samurai fashion as the Americal forces over-ran the island. On a lighter note, the beautiful Motobu Peninsula eighty kilometres from Naha is well worth a visit. A grand International Ocean Exposition was held there in 1975 and there is a permanent Marine Life Zoo and a fascinating Marine Aquarium.

It is quite easy to take short air-flights to other islands of the archipelago and here you will get the true feel of the beauty and langour of a world that is closer in temperament, climate and culture to the Pacific south seas than to much of the Japanese mainland. These only half-developed islands are excellent places to buy genuine locally made artifacts. Colourful textiles, hand-painted and produced by a kind of batik technique, are delightful and so is bashofu cloth made from banana-tree fibres. Ceramics, lacquerware, objects made of coral and tortoise-shell are also produced using different, traditionally Okinawan designs.

A return to Fukuoka from Nara will again put you on the main route for seeing all that Kyushu has to offer, and you can fly from there to Nagasaki. If you have time however, make the Fukuoka-Nagasaki trip by train from which you will see the delightful views of Omura Bay en route. Nagasaki, which now has a population of about half a million, was first opened to foreign trade in 1517. It has long been a favourite with foreigners—except perhaps with those few Dutch traders who were allowed to remain there after all other nationalities were expelled from the country in the early seventeenth century. The Hollanders had a pretty miserable time, for they were penned in leper-like seclusion on the small island of Decima in Nagasaki Bay. They were allowed to leave just once a year, under heavy escort, when they conducted a limited but lucrative trade with merchants of the Shogun's government. The woodblock prints of the period which depict in startling detail how comic and ungainly these 'red-haired barbarians' appeared to the native artists should be examined thoughtfully by anyone interested in the development of relations between the West and Japanese.

The port of Nagasaki is most pleasantly situated on wooded hills beside a deep inlet of the bay and its lineaments of growth can still just be seen. Many of the older buildings along the Bund and in the commercial district were destroyed in 1945 however, when the city was atom-bombed. Only a few reminders of the tragedy remain, for Nagasaki seems to have forgotten the whole dreadful event more completely than has Hiroshima, which was bombed three days earlier. In any case and like Hiroshima, Nagasaki has been completely rebuilt. It is now a thriving centre of commercial and industrial activity and has many new unattractive housing developments that provide cramped homes for the influx of workers.

To appreciate just how serene and picturesque the place must have looked in its earlier days, go first to the old British-style Glover mansion on the hill. During the nineteenth century it was built by an English merchant, Thomas Glover who was quite an energetic figure on the local scene. He was reputed to have enjoyed a vaguely illicit connection with a lady later celebrated as Madame Butterfly, the heroine of Puccini's opera which is set in the port. The opera, incidentally, is based on a little-known story by an American, John Luther Long. The connection between the real Mr Glover and the fictional Madame Butterfly is flimsy indeed; but from the garden of Glover's residence there are splendid views over the hills and the harbour below.

Other and earlier vestiges of Nagasaki's colourful history can be seen in various spots that are on the well-worn tourist tracks. In Nishizaka Park there is a Memorial Hall consecrated to the Japanese and foreign Christians who were martyred in the neighbourhood in 1597 when the 'foreign religion' was persecuted and outlawed by a suspicious shogunate. At the city's main hillside park there are memorial slabs dedicated to two distinguished German scholars and scientists, Engelbert Kaemfer (1651-1776) and Philipp van Siebold (1786-1866). They both lived for brief periods in the country and wrote two of the only comprehensive surviving foreign accounts of Japan as it really was in the eighteenth and early nineteenth centuries.

Splendid evidence of the long-term presence of other foreigners in the port can be seen at the Sofukuji temple, which is an extraordinarily fine example of Chinese temple architecture built in the early seventeenth century. Members of the resident Chinese community still go there to mark their days of religious festival. The Oura Catholic church is now designated as a National Treasure because it was built by a French missionary in 1865 and is the oldest wooden church of Gothic architecture in the land.

Nagasaki is not all historical monuments of course and indeed has long been famed for its colourful and cosmopolitan entertainment and bar quarter which has been a mecca for generations of foreign sailors. When Pierre Loti, the French sailor turned writer, re-visited the port at the turn of the century he lamented that bars reeking with absinthe and gin, rowdy brothels and clattering tramcars had destroyed the quiet charms of the wooden tea-houses and lantern-lit alleys that he had enjoyed visiting twenty years before.

The noise, the bustle and the bars are still there and neon-lights glitter along the shopping streets. There are many good restaurants too, especially Chinese and Korean. One of the most famous is the Kagetsu, which is almost a tourist attraction in its own right. It was created in the eighteenth century in a strange mix of oriental and occidental styles and its main clientèle were outward-looking Japanese who, forbidden to travel abroad, went there to satisfy their yen for the overseas exotic. The local tourist board lays on evening excursions round the gay quarters and sightseeing tours by boat round the harbour and docks. There are also day-excursions to several pleasant spots in the hinterlands, especially to Mogi, a port town noted for its production of the exotic loquat.

From Nagasaki there is what the Japanese (who have rather too enthusiastically adopted American travel-jargon) term a 'Scenic Sky-Line Drive' of about two hours duration to Unzen National Park on the Shimabara Peninsula. The areas boasts many kilometres of lovely coastline and its most spectacular feature is

Mount Unzen which consists of several extinct volcanic peaks. Equally impressive (if you've not already seen to many of them!) are the geysers in the park from which bursts of boiling water gush continually upwards to a considerable height. The whole area has a national reputation for the quality and effectiveness of its medical hot-springs and is therefore well equipped with hotels. A few of them are elegantly old-fashioned and redolent of rather earlier days, offering opportunities for gin and tonics on the verandahs and quiet games of golf. The best seasons for visiting this huge park are in the spring, when acres of azaleas are in bloom, or early autumn, when the hillsides are aflame with the brilliant Japanese maples.

From Shimabara on the peninsula's east coast it is simple to go by ferry and bus to Kumamoto, Kyushu's third largest city. It is a prosperous commercial centre, pleasantly provincial in character, and well supplied with lots of green open spaces and easy access to various small lake and seaside towns nearby. It is also Kyushu's foremost educational centre and Lafcadio Hearn and several other prominent Western scholars taught in its colleges before the war. Kumamoto castle, originally dating from the sixteenth century, was restored in 1960 and is one of the three most famous in the whole country because of its good state of preservation. Its approach is along a slope of cherry trees and from its upper storeys there are grand views of the surrounding city and the lush countryside beyond. Inside is an interesting museum with displays of ancient weapons, utensils and costumes.

Suizenji Park, on the outskirts of Kumamoto, was laid out as a landscape garden in the seventeenth century and is renowned for its size and its pleasing composition of water, hillocks and buildings. It also features what the Japanese call a 'composition model' of other famous scenic panoramas in the country.

The southernmost place of any size on Kyushu is Kagoshima, another castle town with an exciting history of clan warfare and international contact. To discover something about the life and times of one of the region's most powerful family-clans, the Shimazu, visit the Shoko Shusei Museum which is full of relics relating to the family's long and eventful history. One of its most illustrious members, Nariakira Shimazu who lived in the later nineteenth century, was a firm believer in the ways of the West. He introduced several innovations to his people, such as a telegraph service, cotton spinning equipment and modern armaments.

From Kagoshima one more or less has to go north and the interesting way is through the central Kyushu mountains and the Aso National Park which is dominated by Mount Aso, billed as the world's largest volcanic crater. Unfortunately, it doesn't appear quite that impressive because the huge crater basin (measuring nearly sixteen by twenty-two kilometres) is an amalgam of five separate fissures, only one of which is still at all active. It is both possible and safe to climb up to the crater rim to witness the rising clouds of gas and black smoke and sulphur fumes which are regularly emitted from the active crater called Nakadake. The best vantage point for viewing the whole volcanic extent of these rather disquieting natural spectacles is said to be Daikambo Peak.

If the smell of sulphur and the sight of hot water jumping about still appeal, go on to the famous spa of Beppu, where, the Japan Tourist Board claims, an average of 100,000 kilolitres of hot water boil up every day from 3,795 different openings. There are even hot sandbaths on the beach here in which the people bury themseleves as a change from the waters. Beppu's boiling ponds called 'hells' bubble with waters of various hues and are hideously fascinating, especially the bright red ones. As a change from so much violent volcanic activity, it is pleasant to visit the nearby safari park where a varied collection of wild animals from all parts of Asia can be seen living in fairly natural environments.

13 A VENTURE TO THE NORTH

The majority of foreign visitors to Japan head, naturally enough, for the principal objects of tourist interest that are situated within easy reach of the capital, and then go southwards. Only a small proportion venture to the north of Honshu called Tohoku and further yet to the northernmost island of Hokkaido. Generally speaking these priorities are correct, but nevertheless the north is well worth exploring by those who are seeking the experience of a different Japan—the part that has always been the least affected by foreign incursions and presences, both oriental and occidental. So, this part of the country is more provincial, less industrially developed, less sophisticated—the Japanese used to call Tohoku 'Michinoku', which means 'The Back Country'. But, if you have a taste for the wide, cool open spaces and wooded heights of northern landscapes, then it is the way to go.

Owing to the later development of the north, there are fewer good paved roads and very few Western-style hotels outside the cities. But Japanese inns are plentiful and fairly moderately priced compared to those of the south. However, a stay in these during the winter months can only be recommended to the very hardy. It is useless, even for lovers of the old and quaint, to pretend that the traditional methods of heating the indoors (mainly consisting of the small portable charcoal brazier) are adequate—even by British standards. Winter temperatures are severe, and most people prefer to visit any part of north Japan between May and September. However, if you are a devotee of winter sports, you will find that facilities for these are improving every year, for the area is now enjoying a domestic travel boom, and an increasing number of Tokyo-based citizens head north for skiing breaks, especially around the New Year.

Tohoku, north Japan

The administrative and cultural centre of Tohoku is the well laid-out city of Sendai, which is surrounded by low, wooded hills. It doesn't have a great deal to offer in the way of historical interest, though it has long been noted for its prestigious centres of learning. It was severely damaged during World War II so that much of its centre is modern urban blocks; its new shopping arcades display fascinating collections of the arts and crafts traditional to the region—lacquer and copperware in particular, patterned textiles, and the painted wooden Kokeshi dolls that are internationally known and loved. Another odd local product is articles made of umoregi, a type of black lignite.

The most rewarding excursion to make from Sendai is to Matsushima, a bay on the nearby Pacific which is most delightfully dotted with pine-clad islets. Their natural growth and volcanic rocks have been eroded by the violent elements into weird formations that look grotesque—or pleasing, depending on your view. The Japanese are very fond of them, and if you go on an organised tour, you will undoubtedly be taken to the 'Four Grand Sights of Matsushima'—the best vantage points from which to view this unusual panorama. There is, incidentally, an odd little museum in the town of Matsushima where archeological relics and products of the locality are on display.

There are two overland routes north from Sendai to Aomori. The quickest and more straightforward is via the rather nondescript city of Marioka; the longer and more scenic route is west, via the large town of Akita on the Japan Sea coast; the local speciality is woodware made from the cedars that flourish in the vicinity. From there, it is pleasant to go through Towada National Park at the centre of which is a very deep lake that is almost completely circular because its waters cover an extinct volcanic crater. From the quiet little spa villages in the area one can explore the unspoilt landscapes around, either by boat, bus or on foot. An unusual sight at Wainai, near the lake-side resort of Yasumiya is a large trout-hatchery, for this fish is another regional speciality.

From the lake-towns, there are regular bus services to Aomori, the forest-surrounded, lumber-producing city which is the main gateway to the far north and has frequent rail and ferry services to Hokkaido across the water. Hokkaido, formerly called 'Ezo', is the least tamed of Japan's four main islands. It lies on almost the same latitude as central Europe and its climate is often compared to that of south Canada. Although it is the second largest island, it is inhabited by only about five percent of the nation's people and thus there is still a rugged frontier air about it.

About seventy percent of Hokkaido's total area is forested and because of this, and its differences of climate and population density, the agricultural patterns and general way of life have several distinctive features. Quantities of potatoes, oats, sugar beet and flax are grown and an increasing amount of stock farming, mainly of sheep and milch cows, is carried on. In 1971, the government launched a Ten-Year Development Plan designed to improve key industries such as paper-pulp mills, petro-chemicals and iron and steel manufactures. Boosts have also been made to the island's fisheries, for the cold seas around contain abundant harvests of cod, pollack, salmon and king crab. Air and land communications have also been expanded, with a new undersea tunnel linking it to Honshu and modernised airports that allow planes to fly from Tokyo to the island's capital of Sapporo in about an hour.

Before these developments began, Hokkaido was considered to be the absolute back-of-beyond by most southern-based Japanese. And this impression was reinforced by the presence of the Ainu in the land. The Ainu are a rather mysterious people of unknown origin who have no racial or linguistic affiliations with the Japanese mongoloid. They are supposed to have been among the earliest inhabitants of the archipelago, but were steadily pushed northwards by the more dynamic and aggressive Japanese. They are a stocky people of essentially gentle disposition; the men being characterised by thick, black, luxurious moustaches and beards, (hence they are often dubbed 'hairy Ainu'); among the women it was formerly the custom to tattoo themselves around the mouths and wrists. In earlier, undisturbed days, the Ainu lived peaceably in crude thatch huts and their main occupations were fishing, weaving rough cloths from wood-fibres and bear-hunting. The bear was a sacred animal among them and they practised a simple form of nature worship.

Most of the young Ainu of today have been at least partially integrated into the dominant culture of the country through regular school attendance, job-training schemes and increasing contact with the Japanese. There are now only about 17,000 true Ainu left in Hokkaido and their fate is unfortunately similar to that of other endangered human species such as the American Indians. They have become tourist attractions, living in protected villages in or near the National Parks and selling their handmade utensils, craft objects and quaint heirlooms to curious visitors. Two of the best places to see the Ainu as they now live are at Biratori, near Tomikawa in the valley of the Saru River and at Shiraoi, near Lake Shikotsu.

The first city of any real interest in Hokkaido is Hakodate, the

second largest; its attractive natural harbour is a bustle of fishing
activity during the short summer months. Hakodate was first
opened to foreign trade in 1859, along with the other treaty ports,
though for a long while it remained very little developed. Near
the centre, stands a strange-looking building called Goryokaku,
which was Japan's first Western-style fort. It was built in 1864 and
it was here that the remnant-supporters of the Tokugawa
shogunate made their last stand against the imperial forces at the
time of the Meiji restoration in 1868. On the summit of Mount
Hakodate overlooking the city, there's a monument to Thomas
Blakiston, who lived there in considerable isolation from his own
kind for twenty-three years in the late nineteenth century. His
accurate accounts of the little-known species of indigenous birds
and animals were much valued by scientists of his day. Hakodate
also boasts a good museum with exhibits of considerable
archeological, geological and cultural interest and, for the hungry
sightseer, there are a number of restaurants that serve the regional
specialities such as stews made with salmon, crab and several kinds
of shellfish.

From Hakodate there are regular plane and rail connections to
Sapporo, the capital. If you choose the latter method, you will be
within easy reach of two Quasi-National Parks: Onuma, about
eighty percent of which is covered with the waters of deep lakes
and rushing rivers, and Otaru-Niseko with high plateaux and
wonderful coastline views. Later, the railway hugs the shores of
the Pacific and passes through the Shikotsu-Toya National Park
which is a popular resort area much favoured by residents of the
islands two main cities. Its scenery is the usual northern mix of
lakes, mountains and hot-springs and in winter many sports
enthusiasts congregate in the spa of Jozankei where skiing conditions are particularly good.

About a hundred years ago, Sapporo was little more than a
primitive farming settlement. In 1871 the city was laid out and
planned as the capital and in 1886 the government of Hokkaido
was officially established there. The original city plans were
worked out by foreign engineers in the manner of many American
cities, with straight, broad streets intersecting each other at right
angles and a wide, main boulevard through the centre. The names
of its principal streets, such as South First Street and West Third
Avenue have a similarly American ring about them. Naturally,
because of its comparatively recent growth, Sapporo is not rich in
historical buildings or ancient relics, but this thriving metropolis

of just over a million inhabitants has a character very much of its own. There are a number of tree- and flower-lined walkways, plazas with modern statuary displayed in them, and large shopping arcades, some of which are underground because of the extreme winter cold.

The local tourist board organises inspection tours to the different kinds of local sights, such as the Municipal Agricultural Centre, paper-pulp factories, breweries (Sapporo beer has a nationwide reputation) and factories where confectionery is made and dairy products are processed. The most comprehensive collection of Ainu weapons and cultural artifacts in the country is housed in the museum, part of which is dedicated to the redoubtable Dr John Batchelor, a Protestant missionary who travelled by bicycle and horseback during the 1890s distributing Christain tracts and studying the primitive lives of 'the poor benighted heathen Ainu'. There is a well-maintained botanical garden nearby which is part of Sapporo University and has a fine collection of alpine plants and other specimens indigenous to the region. Another place for those with botanical interests is the Maruyama Primeval Forest— registered this time as a Natural Monument. A profusion of plant and tree species grow there, including the cucumber tree.

One of the rewards awaiting those who venture to Sapporo in the winter is the sight of the Yuki Matsuri which is held there every 1 February. It is the largest and most exciting 'Snow Festival' in the country; huge, elaborately carved sculptures made of snow are carried in procession through the streets and there are masses of coloured lanterns, streamers, and a general air of jollity.

Those with a penchant for northern open spaces, crisp clean air and magnificent natural scenery should plan to stay awhile in Hokkaido, for the whole island north of Sapporo is liberally supplied with volcanoes, waterfalls, rushing rivers, conifered valleys, grassy plains and even white-sand and usually empty beaches—many of these contained in one or other of the National Park areas.

The remotest of them all is the park on the Shiretoko Peninsula that juts into the sea of Okhotsk, where the scenery becomes rather bleak and windswept, like the Outer Hebrides. This is about as far as you can go, for over the seas of the northern horizon, the great landmasses of Russia and America begin. Compared to them both, the country called Japan is so very small in size—but not in character or spirit. For, like Britain, it is, in its highly individual way a 'great' country, and offers much to all who visit its shores.

NATIONAL FESTIVALS

1 January	New Year's Day. National holiday. Most places of business closed between 1 and 3 January inclusive.
11 February	National Foundation Day. National holiday celebrating accession to the throne of the first Japanese Emperor, Jimmu.
3 March	Girls' Day. Not a holiday, but widely observed.
20 or 21 March	Vernal Equinox Day. National holiday to celebrate the coming of spring. Visits to ancenstral graves.
29 April	The Emperor's Birthday. National holiday and beginning of 'Golden Week' when most people take the whole week off work.
3 May	Constitution Day. National holiday to commemorate new Constitution.
5 May	Children's Day, formerly called Boys' Day. A national holiday.
15 July approx.	Bon Festival. A day for visiting shrines and local O-Bon dancing. Not national holiday.
23 September	Autumnal Equinox Day. National holiday to celebrate coming of autumn.
10 October	Sports Day. A new national day to commemorate the holding of the Olympics in Tokyo in 1964.
3 November	Culture Day. A national holiday to encourage the people's enjoyment of peace and culture. Formerly the Emperor Meiji's birthday and still remembered as such by many older people.
23 November	Labour Thanksgiving Day. A national holiday of thanksgiving, often combined with harvest festivals. Emperor makes ritual offering of saké to the gods.
24 December	Christmas Eve. A time of celebration and general merriment, some businesses closed. Japanese Christians observe the time by holding church services.

31 December   New Year's Eve. Not a holiday, but time for people to travel and get together with relatives. The bells of important temples ring out 108 times at midnight.

HISTORICAL PERIODS

up to A.D. 600   The Japanese islands were first inhabited by mankind in the later Stone Age, known as the Neolithic. This was followed by the Bronze Age when this material was first introduced from the Asian mainland. These ages merged into the Iron Age when metal weapons etc. were made. Scholars differ as to the exact origins of the Japanese race. Japanese race.

600-784   The Nara period. The social structure was based on family groups. In the seventh century a permanent court was established at Nara and the next seven emperors lived there. The period saw the growth of Buddhism and the artistic culture that was inspired by it.

794-1192   The Heian period. Emperor Kammu (737-806) moved the capital from Nara to a beautiful new site called Heiankyo (later known as Kyoto), so the period is known as the Heian. The period was characterised by further growth and study of Buddhism and of Chinese culture. An era of glory for the imperial house and for various enlightened emperors and empresses. Power and wealth was in the hands of the nobility, but towards the end of the period there was increasing domestic disturbance and discontent in the nation generally.

1192-1333   The Kamakura period. Military-style government founded at Kamakura with powerful new officials in charge of districts and responsible for policing and tax-collecting etc. The period saw the development of military arts and crafts, the martial spirit of the nation and the consolidation of governmental power. Following the Japanese defeat of the Mongol invaders (1281) the

Kamakura shogunate gradually lost financial and political control and the confidence of its warriors. Civil wars followed.

1336-1598   The Muromachi and Azuchi-Momoyama period. Continuation of civil strife characterised this period, during which there were two national capitals for a while, one at Kyoto, another at Yoshino. Power struggles were between the various shoguns and the clans who supported them and these continued for over a hundred years. Culturally, Zen Buddhism was in the ascendant and architecture of a religious kind flourished. Towards the end of the period, Nobunaga Oda and Hideyoshi Toyotomi started to unify and pacify the country and built castle strongholds.

1603-1867   The Edo or Tokugawa period. Shogunate rule was consolidated by Ieyasu Tokugawa; his capital established at Edo (later Tokyo). Expulsion of foreign missionaries from Japan; time of Japanese seclusion from the rest of the world. Culturally, a rich period of growth in the visual and theatrical arts. Towards the end of the period the populace were increasingly restive due to threats of foreign invasion and the repressive policies of the later shoguns. The historic arrival of Commodore Matthew Perry in 1853 signalled the end of Japan's exclusion and the overthrow of the shogunate by a return to imperial power.

1868-1912   The Meiji period. The restoration of Emperor Meiji to the throne was the beginning of Japan's rapid period of modernisation and the dominance of Western influence. Feudal institutions were swept away and Western ideas of democracy and parliamentary government were adopted. The Japanese fought two international wars during the period, against China (1894-5) and against Russia (1904-5). Their victories in these wars and rapid command of military skills increased their stature in the world. Culturally, much was adopted from the West, but in the later part of the period there was renewed interest in native arts and crafts.

1912-   The Taisho and Showa period. The rule of Emperor Taisho (1912-26) saw the rapid expansion of Japan's military and naval power in Asia. In 1937 armed conflicts broke out between the Japanese and Chinese. Culturally, it was a fairly dormant period and the emphasis was on patrotism and the military virtues. The early rule of the present Emperor Hirohito was marked by the country's defeat in World War II and the American occupation. The last twenty years have seen Japan's increasing economic and industrial expansion.

BIBLIOGRAPHY

Arnott, P. *The Theatre of Japan* 1969.
Barr, P. *The Coming of the Barbarians,* 1967.
    The Deer Cry Pavilion, 1968.
Beasley, W. G. *The Modern History of Japan,* 1974.
Benedict, R. *The Chrysanthemum and the Sword,* 1967.
Brandon, J. R. *Five Kabuki Plays* (trans.), 1975.
Endo, Shusako *The Sea and Poison* (F), (trans.) 1972.
        Silence (F) (trans.), 1976.
        Volcano (F) (trans.), 1978.
Ernst, E. *Kabuki Theatre,* 1956.
Hearn, L. *Japan, an Interpretation,* 1904.
Henderson, H. *Introduction to Haiku,* 1958.
Hibbett, H. *Floating World in Japanese Fiction,* 1959.
Hayashiya, T. *Japanese Arts and Tea Ceremony* (trans.), 1974.
Keene, D. *Landscapes and Portraits* (Japanese culture), 1972.
Keene, D. *World within Walls* (pre-modern Japanese Literaure), 1976.
Kennedy, M. *A Short History of Japan,* 1964.
Kirkup, J. *Heaven, Hell and Hara-kiri,* 1974.
Kerr, G. *Okinawa, History of,* 1968.
Morton, W. S. *Japan — history and culture,* 1973.
        New Writing in Japan (Penguin Collection), 1972.
Nish, I. *The Story of Japan,* 1968.
Reischauer, E. *The Japanese,* 1977.
Ross, *The World of Zen,* East-West Anthology, 1962.
Rudofsky, B. *The Kimono Mind,* 1966.
Sansom, G. *Japan, A Cultural History,* 1962 (revised).
Shikibu, Murasaki. *The Tale of Genji* (trans. E. Seidensticker), 1977.
Stewart, H. *A Net of Fireflies* (trans. Haiku), 1960.
Tokutomi, K. *Footprints in the Snow* (F) (trans.), 1970.
Waley, A. *The Noh Plays of Japan* (trans.), 1930.
Wilson, G. and Atsumi, I. *Three Contemporary Japanese Poets* (trans.), 1972.

INDEX